Dr. James

A PLACE CALLED

Home

Inspirations

Tyndale House Publishers, Inc. Wheaton, Illinois

Inspirations is a registered trademark of Tyndale House Publishers, Inc. ■ Copyright ©
1994 by James Dobson, Inc. Psychologist, Professional Corporation. All rights reserved.
International copyright secured. Material quoted is from the following of Dr. Dobson's
Tyndale House books: *Dare to Discipline; Dr. Dobson Answers Your Questions; What
Wives Wish Their Husbands Knew about Women; The Strong-Willed Child; Dr. Dobson
Answers Your Questions about Raising Children; Dr. Dobson Answers Your Questions
about Confident, Healthy Families; Dr. Dobson Answers Your Questions about Marriage
and Sexuality; Preparing for Adolescence; The New Dare to Discipline;* and *When God
Doesn't Make Sense.* ■ Scripture quotations marked TLB are taken from *The Living Bible,*
copyright © 1971 owned by assignment by KNT Charitable Trust. All rights reserved.
Scripture quotations marked KJV are taken from the *Holy Bible,* King James Version.
Scripture quotations marked NIV are from the *Holy Bible,* New International Version®,
copyright © 1973, 1978, 1984 International Bible Society. Used by permission of
Zondervan Publishing House. All rights reserved. The *"NIV"* and *"New International
Version"* trademarks are registered in the United States Patent and Trademark Office by
International Bible Society. ISBN 0-8423-8920-2. Cover illustration copyright © 1993 by
Bradley Clark. All rights reserved. No part of this calendar may be reproduced in any
manner except by written permission of Tyndale House Publishers, Inc. Printed in the
United States of America.

99 98 97 96 95 94
9   8   7   6   5   4   3   2   1

JANUARY 1

New Year's Day

The foundational understanding on which the entire
parent-child relationship rests is found in a careful
balance between love and discipline. The interaction of
those two variables is critical and is as close as we can get
to a formula for successful parenting.

Dr. James Dobson, *The New Dare to Discipline*, p. 48

*Don't be angry when the Lord
punishes you. Don't be discouraged
when he has to show you where you
are wrong. For when he punishes
you, it proves that he loves you.
When he whips you, it proves you are
really his child.* Hebrews 12:5-6 TLB

DECEMBER 31

Parents cannot require their children to treat them with dignity if they will not do the same in return. They should be gentle with their child's ego, never belittling or embarrassing him or her in front of friends.

Dr. James Dobson, *The New Dare to Discipline,* pp. 25–26

In humility consider others better
than yourselves. Each of you should
look not only to your own interests,
but also to the interests of others.
Philippians 2:3-4 NIV

ANUARY 2

Parenthood is a guilty affair. No matter how hard one tries, it is impossible to discharge the responsibility perfectly.

Dr. James Dobson, *What Wives Wish Their Husbands Knew about Women*, p. 159

Jesus replied, "Cases like this require prayer."   Mark 9:29 TLB

DECEMBER 30

Every year that passes should bring fewer rules, less direct discipline, and more independence for the child.

Dr. James Dobson, *The Strong-Willed Child,* p. 61

The Lord grants wisdom! His every word is a treasure of knowledge and understanding. He grants good sense to the godly. Proverbs 2:6-7 TLB

JANUARY 3

Whence cometh the stability in such a topsy-turvy world?
It is found only by anchoring our faith on the unchanging,
everlasting Lord, whose promises never fail and whose
love is all-encompassing.

Dr. James Dobson, *When God Doesn't Make Sense*, pp. 124–125

Everyone who hears these words of
mine and puts them into practice is
like a wise man who built his house
on the rock.   Matthew 7:24 NIV

DECEMBER 29

Heredity does not equip a child with the proper attitudes; children will learn what they are taught. We cannot expect the desirable attitudes and behavior to appear if we have not done our homework.

Dr. James Dobson, *The Strong-Willed Child*, p. 56

Even a child is known by his actions, by whether his conduct is pure and right.   Proverbs 20:11 NIV

January 4

Fortunately, we are permitted to make a few mistakes with our children. No one can expect to do everything right, and it is not the few errors that destroy a child. It is the consistent influence of conditions throughout childhood.

Dr. James Dobson, *The New Dare to Discipline,* pp. 75–76

Praise the LORD, O my soul, and forget not all his benefits—who forgives all your sins and heals all your diseases, who redeems your life from the pit and crowns you with love and compassion. Psalm 103:2-4 NIV

DECEMBER 28

If one examines the secret behind a championship football team, a magnificent orchestra, or a successful business, the principal ingredient is invariably discipline. Adherence to a standard is an important element of discipline.

Dr. James Dobson, *Dare to Discipline,* p. 87

He who ignores discipline comes to poverty and shame, but whoever heeds correction is honored.
Proverbs 13:18 NIV

JANUARY 5

Be absolutely sure your child is capable of delivering what you require. Impossible demands put a boy or girl in an unresolvable conflict: there is no way out. That condition brings inevitable damage to the human emotional apparatus.

Dr. James Dobson, *The Strong-Willed Child,* p. 33

God is faithful; he will not let you be tempted beyond what you can bear. But when you are tempted, he will also provide a way out so that you can stand up under it.
1 Corinthians 10:13 NIV

DECEMBER 27

The accumulation of wealth is an insufficient reason for living.

Dr. James Dobson, *What Wives Wish Their Husbands Knew about Women*, p. 108

What is the advantage of wealth—except perhaps to watch it as it runs through your fingers!
Ecclesiastes 5:11 TLB

JANUARY 6

Families are experiencing an unprecedented period of disintegration which threatens the entire superstructure of our society. We simply must take whatever steps necessary to ensure its integrity.

Dr. James Dobson, *Dr. Dobson Answers Your Questions about Confident, Healthy Families*, p. 11

Any kingdom filled with civil war is doomed; so is a home filled with argument and strife. Luke 11:17 TLB

DECEMBER 26

Loving discipline encourages a child to respect other people and live as a responsible, constructive citizen.

Dr. James Dobson, *The New Dare to Discipline,* p. 7

Live as servants of God. Show proper respect to everyone: Love the brotherhood of believers.
1 Peter 2:16-17 NIV

JANUARY 7

All of us need to know that we are respected for the way
we meet our responsibilities. Men get this emotional
nurture through job promotions, raises in pay, annual
evaluations, and incidental praise during the workday.
Women at home get it from their husbands if they get it at
all.

Dr. James Dobson, *What Wives Wish Their Husbands Knew about Women*, p. 52

We each have different work to do. So
we belong to each other, and each
needs all the others.
                    Romans 12:5 TLB

 # DECEMBER 25

The Creator has given to us parents the awesome
responsibility of representing him to our children. Our
heavenly Father is a God of unlimited love, and our
children must become acquainted with his mercy and
tenderness through our own love toward them.

Dr. James Dobson, *The Strong-Willed Child*, p. 172

Be imitators of God, therefore, as
dearly loved children and live a life of
love, just as Christ loved us and gave
himself up for us as a fragrant
offering and sacrifice to God.
Ephesians 5:1-2 NIV

JANUARY 8

The parent who is most anxious to avoid conflict and confrontation often finds himself screaming and threatening and ultimately thrashing the child. Indeed, child abuse may be the end result.

Dr. James Dobson, *The Strong-Willed Child,* p. 98

And now a word to you parents. Don't keep on scolding and nagging your children, making them angry and resentful. Rather, bring them up with the loving discipline the Lord himself approves, with suggestions and godly advice. Ephesians 6:4 TLB

DECEMBER 24

Proper authority is defined as loving leadership. Without decision-makers and others who agree to follow, there is inevitable chaos and confusion and disorder in human relationships. Loving authority is absolutely necessary for the healthy functioning of a family.

Dr. James Dobson, *The Strong-Willed Child*, p. 179

An elder must be blameless, the husband of but one wife, a man whose children believe and are not open to the charge of being wild and disobedient. Titus 1:6 NIV

JANUARY 9

Raising kids properly is one of life's richest challenges. It is not uncommon to feel overwhelmed by the complexity of the parental assignment.

Dr. James Dobson, *The New Dare to Discipline*, p. 244

I can do everything through him who gives me strength.
Philippians 4:13 NIV

DECEMBER 23

E. L. Thorndike's Law of Reinforcement: Behavior which achieves desirable consequences will recur.

Dr. James Dobson, *Dare to Discipline,* p. 49

Why is your face so dark with rage?
It can be bright with joy if you will do
what you should! But if you refuse to
obey, watch out.   Genesis 4:6 TLB

JANUARY 10

It is obvious that the Creator of the universe is best able to tell us how to raise children, and he has done just that through his Holy Word.

Dr. James Dobson, *Dr. Dobson Answers Your Questions About Raising Children,* p. 70

His divine power has given us
everything we need for life and
godliness through our knowledge of
him who called us by his own glory
and goodness.   2 Peter 1:3 NIV

DECEMBER 22

Many confrontations can be avoided by building friendships with kids and thereby making them want to cooperate at home. It sure beats anger as a motivator!

Dr. James Dobson, *The New Dare to Discipline*, p. 75

May the God who gives endurance and encouragement give you a spirit of unity among yourselves as you follow Christ Jesus, so that with one heart and mouth you may glorify the God and Father of our Lord Jesus Christ.   Romans 15:5-6 NIV

JANUARY 11

We can't afford to abandon our communicative efforts just because parents and teens have difficulty understanding one another. We simply must remain "in touch" during these turbulent years.

Dr. James Dobson, *The Strong-Willed Child*, p. 196

Stay always within the boundaries where God's love can reach and bless you. Jude 1:21 TLB

DECEMBER 21

We should give conscious thought to the reasonable, orderly transfer of freedom and responsibility, so that we are preparing the child each year for the moment of full independence which must come.

Dr. James Dobson, *Dr. Dobson Answers Your Questions About Confident, Healthy Families,* p. 55

My son, how happy I will be if you turn out to be sensible! It will be a public honor to me.

Proverbs 27:11 TLB

JANUARY 12

Anyone who understands children knows that there is a "top dog" in every group, and there is a poor defeated pup at the bottom of the heap.

Dr. James Dobson, *The Strong-Willed Child,* p. 16

Though the Lord is on high, he looks upon the lowly, but the proud he knows from afar. Psalm 138:6 NIV

DECEMBER 20

Children love daily routine activities of the simplest kind.
You can turn the routine chores of living into times of
warmth and closeness if you give a little thought to them.

Dr. James Dobson, *Dr. Dobson Answers Your Questions about Raising Children,* p. 24

Surely goodness and mercy shall
follow me all the days of my life.
Psalm 23:6 KJV

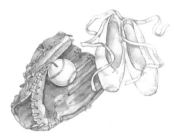

JANUARY 13

What does a hectic pace have to do with depression? Just this: every obligation which we shirk is a source of guilt. When there are more commitments than we can possibly handle, then self-esteem is further damaged by each failure.

Dr. James Dobson, *What Wives Wish Their Husbands Knew about Women*, p. 43

It is senseless for you to work so hard from early morning until late at night, fearing you will starve to death; for God wants his loved ones to get their proper rest.

Psalm 127:2 TLB

DECEMBER 19

Once a child begins to think he's stupid, incapable,
ignorant, or foolish, the concept is not easily eliminated.

Dr. James Dobson, *The New Dare to Discipline*, p. 166

*Are not two sparrows sold for a
penny? Yet not one of them will fall to
the ground apart from the will of
your Father. . . . So don't be afraid;
you are worth more than many
sparrows.* Matthew 10:29, 31 NIV

JANUARY 14

The current epidemic of self-doubt has resulted from a totally unjust and unnecessary system of evaluating human worth now prevalent in our society. It is a cruel system based on beauty and brains. We as parents must counterbalance its impact.

Dr. James Dobson, *Dr. Dobson Answers Your Questions about Healthy, Confident Families*, p. 15

Be beautiful inside, in your hearts,
with the lasting charm of a gentle and
quiet spirit that is so precious to God.
                    1 Peter 3:4 TLB

DECEMBER 18

We serve the Lord not because He dances to our tune, but because we trust His preeminence in our lives. Ultimately, He must be—He *will* be—the determiner of what is in our best interest.

Dr. James Dobson, *When God Doesn't Make Sense,* p. 102

He gave you his rules for daily life so you would know what he wanted you to do. Romans 9:4 TLB

JANUARY 15

One formula applies to all human relationships: the four-letter word called *love*. Conflicts seem to dissolve themselves when people live according to 1 Corinthians 13. The ultimate prescription for harmonious living is contained in that one chapter, and I doubt if any new discovery will ever improve on it.

Dr. James Dobson, *Dr. Dobson Answers Your Questions*, p. 499

These three remain: faith, hope and love. But the greatest of these is love.
1 Corinthians 13:13 NIV

ECEMBER 17

Romantic love [is important] to every aspect of feminine existence. It provides the foundation for a woman's self-esteem, her joy in living, and her sexual responsiveness. Therefore, the vast number of men who are involved in bored, tired marriages—and find themselves locked out of the bedroom—should know where the trouble possibly lies.

Dr. James Dobson, *What Wives Wish Their Husbands Knew about Women,* p. 117

A married man . . . has to think about his earthly responsibilities and how to please his wife.
1 Corinthians 7:33 TLB

JANUARY 16

Children are infinitely complex, and their leadership requires tact, cunning, courage, skill, and knowledge.

Dr. James Dobson, *The Strong-Willed Child,* p. 121

The righteous man leads a blameless life; blessed are his children after him.
Proverbs 20:7 NIV

DECEMBER 16

The will is malleable. It can and should be molded and polished—not to make a robot of a child for our selfish purposes, but to give him the ability to control his own impulses, and exercise self-discipline later in life. In fact, we have a God-given responsibility to shape the will.

Dr. James Dobson, *The Strong-Willed Child*, p. 78

Make every effort to add to your faith goodness; and to goodness, knowledge; and to knowledge, self-control; and to self-control, perseverance; and to perseverance, godliness; and to godliness, brotherly kindness; and to brotherly kindness, love.

2 Peter 1:5-7 NIV

JANUARY 17

There is still no substitute for the biblical prescription for marriage, nor will its wisdom ever be replaced.

Dr. James Dobson, *What Wives Wish Their Husbands Knew about Women*, p. 67

Seek ye first the kingdom of God, and his righteousness; and all these things shall be added unto you.
Matthew 6:33 KJV

DECEMBER 15

We parents, in our great love for our children, can do irreparable harm by yielding to their pleas for more and more things. There are times when the very best reply we can offer is . . . no.

Dr. James Dobson, *The New Dare to Discipline*, p. 48

If you, then, though you are evil,
know how to give good gifts to your
children, how much more will your
Father in heaven give good gifts to
those who ask him!

Matthew 7:11 NIV

JANUARY 18

The central cause of turmoil among the young must again be found in the tender years of childhood; we demanded neither respect nor responsible behavior from our children, and it should not be surprising that some of our young citizens are now demonstrating the absence of these virtues.

Dr. James Dobson, *Dare to Discipline,* p. 12

Honor your father and your mother, as the LORD your God has commanded you, so that you may live long and that it may go well with you in the land the LORD your God is giving you.
Deuteronomy 5:16 NIV

DECEMBER 14

The future of a nation depends on how it sees its women.
I hope we will teach our little girls to be glad they were
chosen by God for the special pleasures of womanhood.

Dr. James Dobson, *What Wives Wish Their Husbands Knew about Women*, p. 35

The Lord God said, "It isn't good for
man to be alone." . . . The Lord God
caused the man to fall into a deep
sleep, and took one of his ribs and
closed up the place from which he had
removed it. . . . "This is it!" Adam
exclaimed. "She is part of my own
bone and flesh! Her name is 'woman'
because she was taken out of a man."
Genesis 2:18, 21, 23 TLB

JANUARY 19

You will not always be saddled with the responsibility you now hold. Your children will be with you for but a few brief years, and the obligations you now shoulder will be nothing more than dim memories. Enjoy every moment of these days—even the difficult times—and indulge yourself in the satisfaction of having done an essential job right!

Dr. James Dobson, *Dr. Dobson Answers Your Questions about Marriage and Sexuality,* p. 45

To enjoy your work and to accept your lot in life—that is indeed a gift from God. The person who does that will not need to look back with sorrow on his past, for God gives him joy.
Ecclesiastes 5:20 TLB

# DECEMBER 13

Love, even genuine love, is a fragile thing. It must be maintained and protected if it is to survive. Love can perish when a husband works seven days a week . . . when there is no time for romantic activity.

Dr. James Dobson, *What Wives Wish Their Husbands Knew about Women*, p. 99

A woman who fears the LORD is to be praised. Give her the reward she has earned. Proverbs 31:30-31 NIV

JANUARY 20

Be willing to let your child experience a reasonable amount of pain or inconvenience when he behaves irresponsibly.

Dr. James Dobson, *The New Dare to Discipline,* p. 116.

Day and night your hand was heavy upon me; my strength was sapped as in the heat of summer. Then I acknowledged my sin to you and did not cover up my iniquity.
                    Psalm 32:4-5 NIV

DECEMBER 12

We adults remember all too clearly the fears and jeers
and tears that represented our own tumultuous youth.
Perhaps that is why parents begin to quake and tremble
when their children approach the adolescent years.

Dr. James Dobson, *The Strong-Willed Child*, p. 189

For God did not give us a spirit of
timidity, but a spirit of power, of love
and of self-discipline.

2 Timothy 1:7 NIV

JANUARY 21

A mother should get out of the house completely for one day a week, doing something for sheer enjoyment. Even if it costs money for a baby sitter, this kind of recreation is more important to the happiness of the home than buying new drapes or a power saw for Dad.

Dr. James Dobson, *What Wives Wish Their Husbands Knew about Women*, p. 53

Come to me and I will give you rest—all of you who work so hard beneath a heavy yoke.
　　　　　Matthew 11:28 TLB

 DECEMBER 11

The wise parent must understand the physical and
emotional characteristics of each stage in childhood, and
then fit the discipline to a boy's or girl's individual needs.

Dr. James Dobson, *The Strong-Willed Child*, p. 39

Yes, if you want better insight and
discernment, and are searching for
them as you would for lost money or
hidden treasure, then wisdom will be
given you and knowledge of God
himself; you will soon learn the
importance of reverence for the Lord
and of trusting him.

Proverbs 2:3-5 TLB

JANUARY 22

Three questions should be asked about every new activity which presents itself: Is it worthy of our time? What will be eliminated if it is added? What will be its impact on our family life? My suspicion is that most of the items in our busy day would score rather poorly on this three-item test.

Dr. James Dobson, *Dr. Dobson Answers Your Questions about Confident, Healthy Families,* p. 85

O Lord, I know it is not within the power of man to map his life and plan his course—so you correct me, Lord; but please be gentle. Don't do it in your anger, for I would die.
Jeremiah 10:23-24 TLB

DECEMBER 10

Many of the emotional problems suffered by some adults can be traced to the viciousness and brutality of siblings and peers during their early home experiences.

Dr. James Dobson, *Dr. Dobson Answers Your Questions,* p. 499

How good and pleasant it is when
brothers live together in unity!
Psalm 133:1 NIV

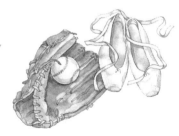

ANUARY 23

Adults should devote their creative energies to the teaching of love and dignity. We should insist that children approach each other with kindness.

Dr. James Dobson, *Dr. Dobson Answers Your Questions about Confident, Healthy Families,* p. 48

A kind man benefits himself, but a cruel man brings trouble on himself.
                    Proverbs 11:17 NIV

DECEMBER 9

The best source of guidance for parents can be found in the wisdom of the Judeo-Christian ethic, which originated with the Creator and was then handed down generation by generation from the time of Christ.

Dr. James Dobson, *The New Dare to Discipline,* p. 16

*I will sing of the LORD's great love
forever; with my mouth I will make
your faithfulness known through all
generations.* Psalm 89:1 NIV

JANUARY 24

Most teenagers respect a guy or girl who has the courage to be his own person, even when being teased.

Dr. James Dobson, *Preparing for Adolescence*, p. 53

You will keep in perfect peace him whose mind is steadfast, because he trusts in you. Trust in the LORD forever, for the LORD, the LORD, is the Rock eternal. Isaiah 26:3 NIV

ECEMBER 8

Self-pity is both addictive and highly contagious. It
spreads like wildfire within a family, neighborhood, or
church congregation.

Dr. James Dobson, *What Wives Wish Their Husbands Knew about Women*, p. 32

*Is God's comfort too little for you? Is
his gentleness too rough?*

Job 15:11 TLB

JANUARY 25

The parent's relationship with his child should be modeled after God's relationship with man. In its ultimate beauty, that interaction is characterized by abundant love—a love unparalleled in tenderness and mercy.

Dr. James Dobson, *The New Dare to Discipline*, p. 248

Because of the LORD's great love we are not consumed, for his compassions never fail. They are new every morning; great is your faithfulness.
Lamentations 3:22-23 NIV

DECEMBER 7

All human behavior is learned—the desirable and the undesirable responses. Children learn to laugh, play, run, and jump; they also learn to whine, bully, pout, fight, throw temper tantrums, or be tomboys. The universal teacher is reinforcement. The child repeats the behavior which he considers to be successful.

Dr. James Dobson, *Dare to Discipline,* p. 53

Be an example to them of good deeds
of every kind.   Titus 2:7 TLB

JANUARY 26

Respect for leadership is the glue that holds social organizations together. Without it there is chaos, violence, and insecurity for everyone. It seems likely that the world is destined to learn this painful lesson once more.

Dr. James Dobson, *Dare to Discipline*, p. 82

Young men, in the same way be submissive to those who are older. . . . Clothe yourselves with humility toward one another, because, "God opposes the proud but gives grace to the humble."   1 Peter 5:5 NIV

DECEMBER 6

Morality and immorality are not defined by man's changing attitudes and social customs. They are determined by the God of the universe, whose timeless standards cannot be ignored without impunity!

Dr. James Dobson, *What Wives Wish Their Husbands Knew about Women*, p. 142

God's laws are perfect. They protect us, make us wise, and give us joy and light. God's laws are pure, eternal, just.   Psalm 19:7-9 TLB

JANUARY 27

Pleasure occurs when an intense need is satisfied. If you never allow a child to want something, he never enjoys the pleasure of receiving it. How unfortunate that such a youngster has never had the chance to long for something, dreaming about it at night and plotting for it by day. The same possession that brought a yawn could have been a trophy and a treasure. I suggest that you allow your child the thrill of temporary deprivation.

Dr. James Dobson, *Dare to Discipline,* p. 31

Whoever loves money never has money enough; whoever loves wealth is never satisfied with his income.
Ecclesiastes 5:10 NIV

DECEMBER 5

Children thrive best in an atmosphere of genuine love, undergirded by reasonable, consistent discipline.

Dr. James Dobson, *Dare to Discipline*, p. 3

May God prosper you and your family and multiply everything you own. 1 Samuel 25:6 TLB

JANUARY 28

A child's will is a powerful force in the human personality.
It is one of the few intellectual components which arrives
full strength at the moment of birth. The will is not
delicate and wobbly.

Dr. James Dobson, *The Strong-Willed Child,* p. 76

*[A father] must manage his own
family well and see that his children
obey him with proper respect.*
1 Timothy 3:4 NIV

DECEMBER 4

One of the purposes of education is to prepare the young for later life. It takes a good measure of self-discipline and control to cope with the demands of modern living.

Dr. James Dobson, *The New Dare to Discipline,* p. 136.

For the grace of God that brings salvation has appeared to all men. It teaches us to say "No" to ungodliness and worldly passions, and to live self-controlled, upright and godly lives in this present age.

Titus 2:11-12 NIV

JANUARY 29

Children cannot raise themselves properly. There is no substitute for loving parental leadership in the early development of children.

Dr. James Dobson, *Dr. Dobson Answers Your Questions about Marriage and Sexuality,* pp. 48–49

The rod of correction imparts wisdom, but a child left to himself disgraces his mother.

Proverbs 29:15 NIV

DECEMBER 3

One should never underestimate a child's awareness that he is breaking the rules. I think most children are rather analytical about their defiance of adult authority; they consider the deed in advance, weighing its probable consequences. If the odds are too great that justice will triumph, they'll take a safer course.

Dr. James Dobson, *Dare to Discipline,* p. 29

The Lord smelled the pleasing aroma and said in his heart: "Never again will I curse the ground because of man, even though every inclination of his heart is evil from childhood. And never again will I destroy all living creatures, as I have done."

Genesis 8:21 NIV

JANUARY 30

A child is fully capable of discerning whether his parent is conveying love or hatred. This is why the youngster who knows he deserves a spanking appears almost relieved when it finally comes. Rather than being insulted by the discipline, he understands its purpose and appreciates the control it gives him over his own impulses.

Dr. James Dobson, *The Strong-Willed Child,* p. 38

We have all had human fathers who disciplined us and we respected them for it. How much more should we submit to the Father of our spirits and live! Hebrews 12:9 NIV

DECEMBER 2

Both a good marriage and a bad marriage have moments of struggle, but in a healthy relationship the husband and wife search for answers and areas of agreement because they love each other.

Dr. James Dobson, *Preparing for Adolescence*, p. 100

Each one of you also must love his wife as he loves himself, and the wife must respect her husband.
Ephesians 5:33 NIV

JANUARY 31

Without an understanding of the justice of our Creator and of our obligations to serve him—and of his promise to punish wickedness—Jesus' death on the cross is of no consequence. He died to provide a remedy for the curse of sin! Unless one understands the curse, the disease, then there is no need for a cure.

Dr. James Dobson, *The Strong-Willed Child*, p. 184

But God commendeth his love toward us, in that, while we were yet sinners, Christ died for us. Romans 5:8 KJV

DECEMBER 1

A mother can expect her child to challenge her authority regularly from the time he is about fifteen months of age, if not earlier. The toddler is the world's most hard-nosed opponent of law and order.

Dr. James Dobson, *Dare to Discipline,* p. 19

I was sinful at birth, sinful from the time my mother conceived me.
Psalm 51:5 NIV

FEBRUARY 1

Don't saturate your child with materialism. There are few conditions that inhibit a sense of appreciation more than for a child to feel he is entitled to whatever he wants, whenever he wants it.

Dr. James Dobson, *The New Dare to Discipline,* pp. 43–44

Command them to do good, to be rich in good deeds, and to be generous and willing to share. In this way they will lay up treasure for themselves.
1 Timothy 6:18-19 NIV

NOVEMBER 30

Why is parental authority so vigorously supported throughout the Bible? The leadership of parents plays a significant role in the development of a child. By learning to yield to the loving authority (leadership) of his parents, a child learns to submit to other forms of authority that will confront him later in life.

Dr. James Dobson, *The Strong-Willed Child,* p. 171

If anyone obeys his word, God's love is truly made complete in him. This is how we know we are in him: Whoever claims to live in him must walk as Jesus did. 1 John 2:5-6 NIV

FEBRUARY 2

Groundhog Day

Each child can be made aware, beyond a shadow of a doubt, that he is a personal creation of God. He can know that the Creator has a plan for his life and that Jesus died for him.

Dr. James Dobson, *Dr. Dobson Answers Your Questions about Raising Children*, p. 26

I know whom I have believed, and am persuaded that he is able to keep that which I have committed unto him against that day.
2 Timothy 1:12 KJV

Money spent on "togetherness" will yield many more benefits than an additional piece of furniture or a new automobile. A woman finds life much more enjoyable if she knows she is the sweetheart, and not just the wife, of her husband.

Dr. James Dobson, *Dare to Discipline*, p. 193

The perfume of your love is more fragrant than all the richest spices. . . . like a private garden, a spring that no one else can have, a fountain of my own.
    Song of Solomon 4:10, 12 TLB

FEBRUARY 3

It would be naive to miss the true meaning of sibling conflict: it often represents a way of manipulating the parents. Quarreling and fighting provide an opportunity for both children to "capture" adult attention. A pair of obnoxious children can tacitly agree to bug their parents until they get a response—even if it is an angry reaction.

Dr. James Dobson, *The Strong-Willed Child*, p. 133

May God who gives patience, steadiness, and encouragement help you to live in complete harmony with each other—each with the attitude of Christ toward the other.

Romans 15:5 TLB

NOVEMBER 28

The parent who intuitively comprehends his child's feelings, thinking his thoughts and seeing life from his perspective, is in a position to respond appropriately and meet the needs that are apparent.

Dr. James Dobson, *The Strong-Willed Child,* p. 121

Which do you choose? Shall I come with punishment and scolding, or shall I come with quiet love and gentleness? 1 Corinthians 4:21 TLB

FEBRUARY 4

An unloved child is truly the saddest phenomenon in all
of nature.

Dr. James Dobson, *Dare to Discipline*, p. 33

Their lives ebb away like those
wounded in battle.
Lamentations 2:12 TLB

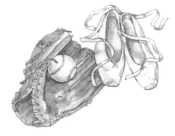

NOVEMBER 27

It is through loving control that parents express personal worth to a child.

Dr. James Dobson, *Dare to Discipline*, p. 39

Good men's sons have a special heritage. Psalm 112:2 TLB

FEBRUARY 5

The issue of what to teach in formal sex education classes is of great importance to the parents who resist society's liberalized attitudes toward sex. The technology of sex is only one component that should be taught. The second critical element involves moral attitudes and the responsibilities related to sex. These components should never be separated! **Dr. James Dobson**, *Dare to Discipline*, p. 149

Cling tightly to your faith in Christ and always keep your conscience clear, doing what you know is right.
1 Timothy 1:19 TLB

The overall objective during the final preadolescent period is to teach the child that his actions have inevitable consequences. One of the most serious casualties in a permissive society is the failure to connect those two factors, behavior and consequences.

Dr. James Dobson, *The Strong-Willed Child,* p. 61

If he sows to please his own wrong desires, he will be planting seeds of evil and he will surely reap a harvest of spiritual decay and death; but if he plants the good things of the Spirit, he will reap the everlasting life that the Holy Spirit gives him.

Galatians 6:8 TLB

FEBRUARY 6

Every move we make directly affects our future, and irresponsible behavior eventually produces sorrow and pain.

Dr. James Dobson, *The New Dare to Discipline*, p. 116

Now that you have been set free from sin and have become slaves to God, the benefit you reap leads to holiness, and the result is eternal life. For the wages of sin is death, but the gift of God is eternal life in Christ Jesus our Lord. Romans 6:22-23 NIV

NOVEMBER 25

Love is not grabbing, or self-centered, or selfish. Real love is being able to contribute to the happiness of another person without expecting to get anything in return.

Dr. James Dobson, *Preparing for Adolescence*, p. 115

Love is patient, love is kind. It does not envy, it does not boast, it is not proud. It is not rude, it is not self-seeking, it is not easily angered, it keeps no record of wrongs.
1 Corinthians 13:4-5 NIV

FEBRUARY 7

The adult who felt unloved or disrespected as a child will *never* fully forget the experience. Childhood inferiority imposes itself on mental apparatus for decades to come.

Dr. James Dobson, *What Wives Wish Their Husbands Knew about Women*, p. 28

Yet there is one ray of hope: his compassion never ends. It is only the Lord's mercies that have kept us from complete destruction. Great is his faithfulness.

Lamentations 3:21-23 TLB

NOVEMBER 24

Where does your marriage rank on your hierarchy of values? Does it get the leftovers and scraps from your busy schedule, or is it something of great worth to be preserved and supported? It can die if left untended.

Dr. James Dobson, *What Wives Wish Their Husbands Knew about Women*, p. 99

A wise woman builds her house, while a foolish woman tears hers down by her own efforts.
　　　　　　Proverbs 14:1 TLB

FEBRUARY 8

It is important to understand the difference between "discipline" and "punishment." Discipline is directed at the objectionable behavior, and the child will accept its consequences without resentment. By contrast, punishment is directed at the individual. As such, . . . it is an expression of hostility, rather than corrective love.

Dr. James Dobson, *Dare to Discipline,* p. 24

Don't fail to correct your children;
discipline won't hurt them!
          Proverbs 23:13 TLB

NOVEMBER 23

The objective is to take the raw material with which our babies arrive on this earth and then gradually mold it into mature, responsible, and God-fearing adults.

Dr. James Dobson, *The New Dare to Discipline,* p. 34

In all my prayers for all of you, I always pray with joy . . . being confident of this, that he who began a good work in you will carry it on to completion until the day of Christ Jesus. Philippians 1:4, 6 NIV

FEBRUARY 9

Nothing builds a woman's self-esteem more effectively
than for a husband to let her (and others) know that he
respects and values her as a person.

Dr. James Dobson, *What Wives Wish Their Husbands Knew about Women*, p. 101

*Live happily with the woman you
love through the fleeting days of life,
for the wife God gives you is your
best reward down here for all your
earthly toil.*   Ecclesiastes 9:9 TLB

NOVEMBER 22

There must be times when God also feels our intense pain and suffers along with us. Wouldn't that be characteristic of a Father whose love was infinite? How He must hurt when we say in confusion, "How could You do this terrible thing, Lord?" . . . How can He explain within our human limitations that . . . there are answers to the tragedies of life?

Dr. James Dobson, *When God Doesn't Make Sense*, p. 62

I will not abandon you or leave you as orphans in the storm—I will come to you. John 14:18 TLB

FEBRUARY 10

Do you want to help your children reach the maximum potential that lies within them? Then raise them according to the precepts and values given to us in the Scriptures.

Dr. James Dobson, *Dr. Dobson Answers Your Questions about Raising Children,* p. 70

This has been my practice: I obey your precepts. Psalm 119:56 NIV

NOVEMBER 21

Our objective as parents should be to do *nothing* for boys and girls which they can profit from doing for themselves.

Dr. James Dobson, *The Strong-Willed Child*, p. 218

Lord, I am overflowing with your blessings, just as you promised. Now teach me good judgment as well as knowledge. Psalm 119:65-66 TLB

FEBRUARY 11

From Genesis to Revelation, there is consistent foundation on which to build an effective philosophy of parent-child relationships.

Dr. James Dobson, *The New Dare to Discipline,* p. 250

*But thanks be to God that, though
you used to be slaves to sin, you
wholeheartedly obeyed the form of
teaching to which you were entrusted.*
Romans 6:17 NIV

The entire human race is afflicted with a strong tendency toward willful defiance. Perhaps this tendency toward self-will is the essence of "original sin". . . . It certainly explains why I place such stress on the proper response to willful defiance during childhood, for that rebellion can yield personal disaster during the troubled days of adolescence.

Dr. James Dobson, *The Strong-Willed Child*, p. 18

[God] is especially hard on those who follow their own evil, lustful thoughts, and those who are proud and willful, daring even to scoff at the Glorious Ones without so much as trembling.
2 Peter 2:10 TLB

 EBRUARY 12   *Lincoln's Birthday*

While yielding to the loving leadership of their parents,
children are also learning to yield to the benevolent
leadership of God himself.

Dr. James Dobson, *The Strong-Willed Child,* p. 171

He shall turn the heart of the fathers
to the children, and the heart of the
children to their fathers.
                    Malachi 4:6 KJV

NOVEMBER 19

Children derive security from knowing where the
boundaries are and who's available to enforce them.

Dr. James Dobson, *The New Dare to Discipline*, p. 59

*The name of the LORD is a strong
tower; the righteous run to it and are
safe.* Proverbs 18:10 NIV

FEBRUARY 13

Genuine love is focused on another human being. It brings a deep desire to make that person happy . . . to meet their needs and satisfy their desires and protect their interests. Real love is best described as being unselfish in all aspects, even if a personal sacrifice is required in the relationship.

Dr. James Dobson, *Preparing for Adolescence*, p. 97

Love does not delight in evil but rejoices with the truth. It always protects, always trusts, always hopes, always perseveres. Love never fails.
1 Corinthians 13:6-8 NIV

NOVEMBER 18

A successful husband-and-wife relationship begins with the attitude of the man; he has been ordained by God as the head of the family, and the responsibility for its welfare rests on his shoulders.

Dr. James Dobson, *What Wives Wish Their Husbands Knew about Women*, p. 67

Godly men are growing a tree that bears life-giving fruit.
Proverbs 11:30 TLB

FEBRUARY 14

Valentine's Day

Real love can melt an iceberg.

Dr. James Dobson, *What Wives Wish Their Husbands Knew about Women,* p. 117

Your godly lives will speak to them
better than any words.
                    1 Peter 3:2 TLB

Children love good disciplinarians primarily because they are afraid of each other and want the security of a leader who can provide a safe atmosphere. Anything can happen in the absence of adult leadership.

Dr. James Dobson, *The Strong-Willed Child*, p. 87

The fruit of righteousness will be peace; the effect of righteousness will be quietness and confidence forever. My people will live in peaceful dwelling places, in secure homes, in undisturbed places of rest.
Isaiah 32:17-18 NIV

EBRUARY 15

The healthiest marriages are those where the couple has learned *how* to fight— how to ventilate anger without tearing one another apart. Healthy conflict focuses on the issue. Personal comments are damaging.

Dr. James Dobson, *Dr. Dobson Answers Your Questions*, p. 330

If you are angry, don't sin by nursing your grudge. Don't let the sun go down with you still angry—get over it quickly; for when you are angry you give a mighty foothold to the devil. Ephesians 4:26 TLB

NOVEMBER 16

Children are like clocks; they must be allowed to run.

Dr. James Dobson, *The Strong-Willed Child*, p. 161

*In everything you do, put God first,
and he will direct you and crown
your efforts with success.*
        Proverbs 3:6 TLB

FEBRUARY 16

Self-esteem is the most fragile attribute in human nature.
It can be damaged by very minor incidents, and its
reconstruction is often difficult to engineer.

Dr. James Dobson, *The New Dare to Discipline,* p. 26

*Do not let any unwholesome talk
come out of your mouths, but only
what is helpful for building others up
according to their needs, that it may
benefit those who listen.*
Ephesians 4:29 NIV

NOVEMBER 15

Disciplinary action influences behavior; anger does not. As a matter of fact, I am convinced that adult anger produces a destructive kind of disrespect in the minds of our children. They perceive that our frustration is caused by our inability to control the situation.

Dr. James Dobson, *The Strong-Willed Child,* p. 100

Refrain from anger and turn from wrath; do not fret—it leads only to evil.   Psalm 37:8 NIV

FEBRUARY 17

Children can't grow without taking risks. Toddlers can't walk initially without falling down. Students can't learn without facing some hardships. And, ultimately, an adolescent can't enter young adulthood until we release him from our protective custody.

Dr. James Dobson, *Dr. Dobson Answers Your Questions about Confident, Healthy Families,* p. 56

My son, how I will rejoice if you become a man of common sense. Yes, my heart will thrill to your thoughtful, wise words.
Proverbs 23:15-16 TLB

NOVEMBER 14

Even genuine love between a man and a woman is vulnerable to pain and trauma; it often wobbles when assaulted by life.

Dr. James Dobson, *What Wives Wish Their Husbands Knew about Women*, p. 95

Carry each other's burdens, and in this way you will fulfill the law of Christ. Galatians 6:2 NIV

FEBRUARY 18

Many behavioral problems can be prevented by simply avoiding the circumstances that create them. Parents can head off many problems by simply "managing" a child's activities and social involvements. The key here is to "think ahead"!

Dr. James Dobson, *The Strong-Willed Child,* p. 65

Run from anything that gives you the evil thoughts that young men often have, but stay close to anything that makes you want to do right.
2 Timothy 2:22 TLB

NOVEMBER 13

The obvious hope is that the adolescent will respect and
appreciate his parents enough to believe what they say
and accept what they recommend.

Dr. James Dobson, *The New Dare to Discipline,* p. 228

Be sure to fear the LORD and serve
him faithfully with all your heart;
consider what great things he has
done for you. 1 Samuel 12:24 NIV

FEBRUARY 19

[God] is not our servant—we are His. And our reason for existence is to glorify and honor Him. Even so, sometimes he performs mighty miracles on our behalf. Sometimes He chooses to explain His action in our lives. . . . But at other times when nothing makes sense . . . He simply says, "Trust Me!"

Dr. James Dobson, *When God Doesn't Make Sense,* p. 41

Blessings on all who reverence and trust the Lord—on all who obey him! Their reward shall be prosperity and happiness. Psalm 128:1-2 TLB

NOVEMBER 12

The overriding principle of parenting remains the same: it involves discipline with love, a reasonable introduction to responsibility and self-control, parental leadership with a minimum of anger, respect for the dignity and worth of the child, realistic boundaries that are enforced with confident firmness, and a judicious use of rewards and punishment to those who challenge and resist.

Dr. James Dobson, *The Strong-Willed Child,* p. 112

Be wise: make the most of every
opportunity you have for doing good.
Ephesians 5:16 TLB

FEBRUARY 20

Life inevitably brings pain and sorrow to little people, and we hurt when they hurt. We want to rise like a mighty shield to protect them from life's sting—to hold them snugly within the safety of our embrace. Yet there are times when we must let them struggle. Children can't grow without taking risks.

Dr. James Dobson, *The Strong-Willed Child,* p. 218

For we do not have a high priest who is unable to sympathize with our weaknesses, but we have one who has been tempted in every way, just as we are—yet was without sin.
Hebrews 4:15 NIV

NOVEMBER 11

Veterans Day

Love must be supported and fed and protected, just like a little infant who is growing up at home.

Dr. James Dobson, *Preparing for Adolescence*, p. 114

Speaking the truth in love, we will in all things grow up into him who is the Head, that is, Christ. From him the whole body, joined and held together by every supporting ligament, grows and builds itself up in love.
Ephesians 4:15-16 NIV

FEBRUARY 21

No job can compete with the responsibility of shaping
and molding a new human being..

Dr. James Dobson, *What Wives Wish Their Husbands Knew about Women*, p. 165

*Jotham . . . did what was right in the
eyes of the Lord, just as his father
Uzziah had done.*
2 Chronicles 27:1-2 NIV

NOVEMBER 10

The chasm between generations does not develop from a failure to communicate; our difficulties result more from what we *do* understand in our communication than in our confusion with words. The conflict between generations occurs because of a breakdown in mutual respect, and it bears painful consequences.

Dr. James Dobson, *Dare to Discipline,* p. 15

"Honor your father and mother"— which is the first commandment with a promise—"that it may go well with you and that you may enjoy long life on the earth." Ephesians 6:2-3 NIV

FEBRUARY 22

Washington's Birthday

The way a child sees his parents' leadership sets the tone for his eventual relationships with his teachers, school principal, police, neighbors, and employers. And ultimately, of course, respect of earthly authority teaches children to yield to the benevolent authority of God himself.

Dr. James Dobson, *Dr. Dobson Answers Your Questions about Raising Children,* p. 124

After this I heard the shouting of a vast crowd in heaven, "Hallelujah! Praise the Lord! Salvation is from our God. Honor and authority belong to him alone." Revelation 19:1 TLB

NOVEMBER 9

Discipline requires courage, consistency, conviction, diligence, and enthusiastic effort.

Dr. James Dobson, *Dare to Discipline,* p. 4

*The wisdom that comes from heaven
is first of all pure; then peace-loving,
considerate, submissive, full of mercy
and good fruit, impartial and sincere.*
James 3:17 NIV

FEBRUARY 23

Adolescence is a condensation or composite of all the training and behavior that has gone before. Any unsettled turbulence in the first twelve years is likely to fester and erupt during adolescence.

Dr. James Dobson, *Dare to Discipline,* p. 21

Speak to each other about these things every day while there is still time, so that none of you will become hardened against God, being blinded by the glamor of sin.

Hebrews 3:13 TLB

NOVEMBER 8

Men and women should recognize that dissatisfaction with life can become nothing more than a bad habit—a costly attitude that can rob them of life's pleasures.

Dr. James Dobson, *The New Dare to Discipline,* p. 246

*I have learned the secret of being
content in any and every situation,
whether well fed or hungry, whether
living in plenty or in want.*
Philippians 4:12 NIV

FEBRUARY 24

We are vulnerable to the slightest frustration, because we have been taught that troubles can be avoided. We have permitted our emotions to rule us, and in so doing, have become mere slaves to our feelings.

Dr. James Dobson, *Dr. Dobson Answers Your Questions about Confident, Healthy Families*, p. 88

He replied, "You are talking like a foolish woman. Shall we accept good from God, and not trouble?" In all this, Job did not sin in what he said.
                    Job 2:10 NIV

NOVEMBER 7

A teenager is often desperately in need of respect and dignity. Give him these gifts.

Dr. James Dobson, *The Strong-Willed Child,* p. 190

For thou hast . . . crowned him with glory and honour. Psalm 8:5 KJV

FEBRUARY 25

Two distinct messages must be conveyed to every child during his first forty-eight months: (1) "I love you more than you can possibly understand" and (2) "Because I love you I must teach you to obey me."

Dr. James Dobson, *Dr. Dobson Answers Your Questions about Raising Children,* p. 16

Children, obey your parents; this is the right thing to do because God has placed them in authority over you.
Ephesians 6:1 TLB

NOVEMBER 6

It is important to know that you have to work to keep love alive; you have to protect it and maintain it, just like you would a delicate flower.

Dr. James Dobson, *Preparing for Adolescence*, p. 96

Let love be your greatest aim.
1 Corinthians 14:1 TLB

FEBRUARY 26

If you love something, set it free. If it comes back to you, then it's yours. If it doesn't return, then it never was yours in the first place.

Dr. James Dobson, *The Strong-Willed Child*, p. 220

Many waters cannot quench the flame of love, neither can the floods drown it. If a man tried to buy it with everything he owned, he couldn't do it.
Song of Solomon 8:7 TLB

NOVEMBER 5

Grandparents probably should not punish their grandkids unless the parents have given them permission to do so.

Dr. James Dobson, *The New Dare to Discipline*, p. 63

Listen to advice and accept instruction, and in the end you will be wise. Proverbs 19:20 NIV

FEBRUARY 27

There will be occasions when we will pray for the will of God to be known, yet hear no immediate reply. We need to understand, however, that God is as close to us and as involved in our situation during those times as he is when we are spiritually exhilarated.

Dr. James Dobson, *Dr. Dobson Answers Your Questions,* p. 486

We are pressed on every side by troubles, but not crushed and broken. We are perplexed because we don't know why things happen as they do, but we don't give up and quit. We are hunted down, but God never abandons us. 2 Corinthians 4:8-9 TLB

NOVEMBER 4

Bitterness and resentment are emotional cancers that rot us from within.

Dr. James Dobson, *Dr. Dobson Answers Your Questions about Confident, Healthy Families*, p. 72

Look after each other so that not one of you will fail to find God's best blessings. Watch out that no bitterness takes root among you, for as it springs up it causes deep trouble, hurting many in their spiritual lives.
Hebrews 12:15 TLB

FEBRUARY 28

We can make no greater mistake as a nation than to devalue the importance of the home and the sustenance which children should be given there.

Dr. James Dobson, *What Wives Wish Their Husbands Knew about Women*, p. 12

Praise her for the many fine things she does. These good deeds of hers shall bring her honor and recognition from people of importance.
Proverbs 31:31 TLB

NOVEMBER 3

A woman's emotional investment in her home usually exceeds that of her husband. She typically cares more about the minor details of the house, family functioning, and such concerns.

Dr. James Dobson, *Dr. Dobson Answers Your Questions about Marriage and Sexuality,* p. 66

A wife of noble character who can find? She is worth far more than rubies. Her husband has full confidence in her and lacks nothing of value. She brings him good, not harm, all the days of her life.
Proverbs 31:10-12 NIV

FEBRUARY 29

A boy or girl who knows love abounds at home will not resent well-deserved punishment. One who is unloved or ignored will hate any form of discipline!

Dr. James Dobson, *The New Dare to Discipline,* p. 62

No discipline seems pleasant at the time, but painful. Later on, however, it produces a harvest of righteousness and peace for those who have been trained by it. Hebrews 12:11 NIV

NOVEMBER 2

The parent who loves her cute little butterball so much that she cannot risk antagonizing him may lose and never regain his control.

Dr. James Dobson, *Dare to Discipline*, p. 20

Honoring a rebel will backfire like a stone tied to a slingshot!
            Proverbs 26:8 TLB

MARCH 1

If you want your child to respect your values in his teen years then you must be worthy of his respect during his younger days.

Dr. James Dobson, *Dare to Discipline*, p. 15

Don't let anyone think little of you because you are young. Be their ideal; let them follow the way you teach and live; be a pattern for them in your love, your faith, and your clean thoughts.   1 Timothy 4:12 TLB

NOVEMBER 1

Jesus made it clear that there is a direct relationship between materialism and spiritual poverty. Accordingly it is my belief that excessive materialism in parents has the power to inflict enormous spiritual damage on our sons and daughters. If they see that we care more about things than people, the result is often cynicism and disbelief.

Dr. James Dobson, *Dr. Dobson Answers Your Questions about Raising Children,* p. 47

Your riches won't help you on Judgment Day; only righteousness counts then. . . . Trust in your money and down you go! Trust in God and flourish as a tree!

Proverbs 11:4, 28 TLB

MARCH 2

Three questions should be asked about every new activity that presents itself: (1) Is it worthy of our time? (2) What will be eliminated if it is added? (3) What will be its impact on our family life?

Dr. James Dobson, *What Wives Wish Their Husbands Knew about Women*, p. 54

Teach us to·number our days and recognize how few they are; help us to spend them as we should.
Psalm 90:12 TLB

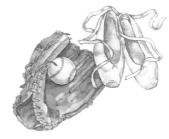

CTOBER 31

Reformation Day

Children should also be taught ultimate loyalty to God.

Dr. James Dobson, *The New Dare to Discipline,* p. 228

They will be my people, and I will be their God. I will give them singleness of heart and action, so that they will always fear me for their own good and the good of their children after them. Jeremiah 32:38-39 NIV

MARCH 3

There is comfort to be found in making a list of the duties to be performed. . . . You can guarantee that the most important jobs will get done first. And you have the satisfaction of crossing tasks off the list as they are completed. When the day is thus ended, then lay the heavy burden at the feet of the Master and rest in knowing you did the best you could.

Dr. James Dobson, *Dare to Discipline,* p. 195

They that wait upon the Lord shall renew their strength. They shall mount up with wings like eagles; they shall run and not be weary; they shall walk and not faint. Isaiah 40:31 TLB

OCTOBER 30

We live in a very hectic period of American history, where fatigue and time pressure are our worst enemies.

Dr. James Dobson, *The Strong-Willed Child*, p. 137

Let us fix our eyes on Jesus, the author and perfecter of our faith, who for the joy set before him endured the cross, scorning its shame, and sat down at the right hand of the throne of God. Consider him who endured such opposition from sinful men, so that you will not grow weary and lose heart. Hebrews 12:2-3 NIV

MARCH 4

The right to criticize must be earned, even if the advice is constructive in nature. Before you are entitled to tinker with another person's self-esteem, you are obligated first to demonstrate your own respect for him as a person.

Dr. James Dobson, *Dr. Dobson Answers Your Questions about Confident, Healthy Families,* p. 73

Reckless words pierce like a sword,
but the tongue of the wise brings
healing. Proverbs 12:18 NIV

OCTOBER 29

I see small children as vulnerable little creatures who need buckets of love and tenderness every day of their lives.

Dr. James Dobson, *The Strong-Willed Child*, p. 73

Hope does not disappoint us, because God has poured out his love into our hearts by the Holy Spirit, whom he has given us. Romans 5:5 NIV

MARCH 5

It is impossible to shield youth from the permissive attitudes that are prevalent today. Television brings every aspect of sexual gratification into the sanctuary of one's living room.

Dr. James Dobson, *The New Dare to Discipline,* p. 216

Flee from sexual immorality. All other sins a man commits are outside his body, but he who sins sexually sins against his own body. Do you not know your body is a temple of the Holy Spirit?

1 Corinthians 6:18-19 NIV

OCTOBER 28

Early Mosaic law made it clear that the emotional well-being of the wife is the specific responsibility of her husband. It was his job to "cheer" her. Friends and neighbors, it still is!

Dr. James Dobson, *What Wives Wish Their Husbands Knew about Women*, p. 68

A man . . . shall cheer up his wife which he hath taken.
Deuteronomy 24:5 KJV

MARCH 6

There is no area of the church mission that I feel is weaker
or more ineffective than discipline in the Sunday school.
Children are permitted to throw erasers and shoot paper
wads and swing on the light fixtures. This is particularly
distressing to me. . . . The chaos that results is an insult to
God and to the meaning of worship. You can't teach
anything when the students don't even hear you.

Dr. James Dobson, *The Strong-Willed Child,* p. 186

*God is not one who likes things to be
disorderly and upset. . . . Be sure that
everything is done properly in a good
and orderly way.*
1 Corinthians 14:33, 40 TLB

OCTOBER 27

There is nothing that rejuvenates the parched, delicate spirits of children faster than when a lighthearted spirit pervades the home and laughter fills its halls.

Dr. James Dobson, *The New Dare to Discipline,* p. 67

Thou wilt show me the path of life: in thy presence is fulness of joy; at thy right hand there are pleasures for evermore.   Psalm 16:11 KJV

MARCH 7

Married life offers no panacea—if it is going to reach its potential, it will require an all-out investment by both husband and wife.

Dr. James Dobson, *What Wives Wish Their Husbands Knew about Women*, p. 103

*So, if you think you are standing
firm, be careful that you don't fall!*
1 Corinthians 10:12 NIV

OCTOBER 26

The decline of a marriage is rarely brought about by a blowout; it usually falls victim to a slow leak.

Dr. James Dobson, *What Wives Wish Their Husbands Knew about Women*, p. 82

So be on your guard.
1 Thessalonians 5:6 TLB

MARCH 8

There's no doubt about it, raising children as a single parent is the loneliest job in the world!

Dr. James Dobson, *What Wives Wish Their Husbands Knew about Women*, p. 159

But even so, you love me! You are holding my right hand! You will keep on guiding me all my life with your wisdom and counsel, and afterwards receive me into the glories of heaven!
Psalm 73:23-24 TLB

OCTOBER 25

The parent's attitude toward his disobedient youngster should be this: "I love you too much to let you behave in destructive ways."

Dr. James Dobson, *Dare to Discipline*, p. 18

Everyone who sins breaks the law; in fact, sin is lawlessness. But you know that he appeared so that he might take away our sins. And in him is no sin. No one who lives in him keeps on sinning. 1 John 3:4-6 NIV

ℳARCH 9

The universe is ordered by a supreme Lord who requires obedience from his children and has warned them that the "wages of sin is death." To show our little ones love without authority is as serious a distortion of God's nature as to reveal an iron-fisted authority without love.

Dr. James Dobson, *The Strong-Willed Child,* p. 172

LORD, I have heard of your fame; I stand in awe of your deeds, O LORD. Renew them in our day, in our time make them known; in wrath remember mercy. Habakkuk 3:2 NIV

OCTOBER 24

What's your rush? Don't you know your children will be gone so quickly and you will have nothing but blurred memories of those years when they needed you?

Dr. James Dobson, *What Wives Wish Their Husbands Knew about Women,* pp. 50–51

Man . . . bustles about, but only in vain; he heaps up wealth, not knowing who will get it.

Psalm 39:6 NIV

It is my belief that we have departed from the standard which was clearly outlined in both the Old and New Testaments, and that deviation is costing us a heavy toll in the form of social turmoil. Self-control, human kindness, and peacefulness can again be manifest in America if we dare to discipline in our homes, churches, and schools.

Dr. James Dobson, *Dare to Discipline,* p. 197

Do not think that I have come to abolish the Law or the Prophets; I have not come to abolish them but to fulfill them. Matthew 5:17 NIV

OCTOBER 23

In the matter of sex education, the best approach begins
in early childhood and extends through the years,
according to a policy of openness, frankness, and honesty.
Only parents can provide this lifetime training.

Dr. James Dobson, *The New Dare to Discipline,* p. 217

*My son, keep my words and store up
my commands within you. Keep my
commands and you will live; guard
my teachings as the apple of your eye.*
Proverbs 7:1-2 NIV

MARCH 11

Men derive self-esteem by being respected; women feel
worthy when they are loved.

Dr. James Dobson, *What Wives Wish Their Husbands Knew about Women,* p. 64

*Just as there are many parts to our
bodies, so it is with Christ's body. We
are all parts of it, and it takes every
one of us to make it complete, for we
each have different work to do. So we
belong to each other, and each needs
all the others.*   Romans 12:4-5 TLB

OCTOBER 22

I pledged to Shirley that I would spend the rest of my life trying to provide the kind of happiness and security she had missed as a child. This was the foundation on which our little family was built. . . . We have seen God's consistent faithfulness in response to our prayers. I don't know where we would be without this source of strength and sustenance.

Dr. James Dobson, *When God Doesn't Make Sense,* pp. 99–100

Every morning tell him, "Thank you for your kindness," and every evening rejoice in all his faithfulness.
Psalm 92:2 TLB

MARCH 12

The best preparation for responsible adulthood is derived from training in responsibility during early childhood.

Dr. James Dobson, *Dr. Dobson Answers Your Questions about Confident, Healthy Families*, p. 55

A wise youth makes hay while the sun shines, but what a shame to see a lad who sleeps away his hour of opportunity. Proverbs 10:5 TLB

OCTOBER 21

Physical depletion renders us less able to cope with the noisiness of children, the dishwasher that won't work, and the thousands of other minor irritations of everyday living.

Dr. James Dobson, *What Wives Wish Their Husbands Knew about Women*, p. 44

For in six days the Lord made the heaven, earth, and sea, and everything in them, and rested the seventh day; so he blessed the Sabbath day and set it aside for rest.
Exodus 20:11 TLB

MARCH 13

I don't believe in harsh, inflexible discipline, even when it is well-intentioned. Children must be given room to breathe and grow and love.

Dr. James Dobson, *The Strong-Willed Child*, p. 75

So then, just as you received Christ Jesus as Lord, continue to live in him, rooted and built up in him, strengthened in the faith as you were taught, and overflowing with thankfulness. Colossians 2:6-7 NIV

OCTOBER 20

Parents should introduce their child to discipline and
self-control by the use of external influences when he is
young. By being required to behave responsibly, he gains
valuable experience in controlling his own impulses and
resources.

Dr. James Dobson, *The Strong-Willed Child*, p. 66

*Our fathers disciplined us for a little
while as they thought best; but God
disciplines us for our good, that we
may share in his holiness.*
        Hebrews 12:10 NIV

MARCH 14

Discipline and love are not antithetical; one is a function of the other.

Dr. James Dobson, *Dare to Discipline*, p. 18

The LORD disciplines those he loves,
as a father the son he delights in.
            Proverbs 3:12 NIV

OCTOBER 19

Women yearn to be the special sweethearts of their men, being respected and appreciated and loved with tenderness.

Dr. James Dobson, *What Wives Wish Their Husbands Knew about Women*, p. 65

How beautiful you are and how pleasing, O love, with your delights!
Song of Solomon 7:6 NIV

MARCH 15

There is *nothing* more important to most Christian parents than the salvation of their children. Every other goal and achievement in life is anemic and insignificant compared to this transmission of faith to their offspring.

Dr. James Dobson, *When God Doesn't Make Sense*, pp. 199–200

These are the commands, decrees and laws the LORD your God directed me to teach you to observe . . . so that you, your children and their children after them may fear the LORD your God as long as you live by keeping all his decrees and commands that I give you, and so that you may enjoy long life.
Deuteronomy 6:1-2 NIV

OCTOBER 18

Anything that worries or troubles a child can result in school failure. For example, problems at home or feelings of inadequacy can prevent academic concentration.

Dr. James Dobson, *The New Dare to Discipline,* p. 192

I sought the LORD, and he answered me; he delivered me from all my fears.
Psalm 34:4 NIV

March 16

When a forty-five-pound bundle of trouble can deliberately reduce his powerful mother or father to a trembling, snarling mass of frustrations, then something changes in their relationship. The child develops an attitude of contempt which is certain to erupt during the stormy adolescent years to come.

Dr. James Dobson, *The Strong-Willed Child,* p. 111

I am going to do all of the dreadful things I warned Eli about. I have continually threatened him and his entire family with punishment because his sons are blaspheming God, and he doesn't stop them."
1 Samuel 3:12-13 TLB

OCTOBER 17

Adherence to a standard is an important element of discipline.

Dr. James Dobson, *Dare to Discipline,* p. 87

He gave his laws to Israel and
commanded our fathers to teach
them to their children, so that they in
turn could teach their children too.
               Psalm 78:5-6 TLB

MARCH 17

Crowded lives produce fatigue—and fatigue produces
irritability—and irritability produces indifference—and
indifference can be interpreted by the child as a lack of
genuine affection and personal esteem.

Dr. James Dobson, *Dr. Dobson Answers Your Questions about Raising Children,* p. 22

*The Lord is my shepherd, I shall not
be in want. He makes me lie down in
green pastures, he leads me beside
quiet waters, he restores my soul. He
guides me in paths of righteousness
for his name's sake.*

Psalm 23:1-3 NIV

OCTOBER 16

If we really love others as much as ourselves, we will give as much time and attention to helping them avoid pain and ridicule as we do ourselves.

Dr. James Dobson, *Preparing for Adolescence*, p. 58

"Love the Lord your God with all your heart and with all your soul and with all your strength and with all your mind"; and, "Love your neighbor as yourself."

Luke 10:27 NIV

MARCH 18

The concepts of marriage and parenthood were not human inventions. God created and ordained the family as a basic unit of procreation and companionship. The solutions to the problems of parenthood can be found through the power of prayer and personal appeal to the Great Creator.

Dr. James Dobson, *Dare to Discipline,* p. 195

Glory be to God, who by his mighty power at work within us is able to do far more than we would ever dare to ask or even dream of.
Ephesians 3:20 TLB

OCTOBER 15

Many children who fail in school are merely doing what they think others expect of them. Our reputation with our peers is a very influential force in our lives.

Dr. James Dobson, *The New Dare to Discipline,* p. 178

*Live such good lives among the
pagans that, though they accuse you
of doing wrong, they may see your
good deeds and glorify God.*
1 Peter 2:12 NIV

$\mathcal{M}$ARCH 19

For all the rough edges which can never be smoothed and the faults which can never be eradicated, try to develop the best possible perspective and determine in your mind to accept reality as it is. The first principle of mental health is to accept that which cannot be changed.

Dr. James Dobson, *What Wives Wish Their Husbands Knew about Women*, p. 183

Be kind and compassionate to one
another, forgiving each other, just as
in Christ God forgave you.
                    Ephesians 4:32 NIV

# OCTOBER 14

Treat the late adolescent like an adult; he's more likely to act like one if he is given the status offered to other adults.

Dr. James Dobson, *Dare to Discipline,* p. 101

He began to be in need. . . . But no one gave him anything.
Luke 15:14, 16 NIV

MARCH 20

I cannot overemphasize the importance of parental support and love during the formative years of life. A child's sense of security and well-being is primarily rooted in the stability of his home and family.

Dr. James Dobson, *The Strong-Willed Child*, p. 117

I will not forget you! See, I have engraved you on the palms of my hands; your walls are ever before me.
Isaiah 49:15-16 NIV

OCTOBER 13

Adolescence is not an easy time of life for either generation; in fact, it can be downright terrifying. But the key to surviving this emotional experience is to lay the proper foundation and then face it with courage.

Dr. James Dobson, *The Strong-Willed Child*, p. 222

Be strong and courageous. Do not be terrified; do not be discouraged, for the LORD your God will be with you wherever you go. Joshua 1:9 NIV

$\mathcal{M}$ARCH 21

The solutions to the problems of modern parenthood can be found through the power of prayer and personal appeal to the Creator.

Dr. James Dobson, *The New Dare to Discipline,* p. 247

This is the confidence we have in approaching God: that if we ask anything according to his will, he hears us. 1 John 5:14 NIV

OCTOBER 12

The most unhappy wives and mothers are often those
who handle their fatigue and loneliness in solitude, and
their men are never very sure why they always act so tired.

Dr. James Dobson, *What Wives Wish Their Husbands Knew about Women*, p. 52

*Find rest, O my soul, in God alone;
my hope comes from him. He alone is
my rock and my salvation; he is my
fortress, I will not be shaken.*
Psalm 62:5-6 NIV

What do women most want from their husbands? It is the assurance that "hand in hand we'll face the best and worst that life has to offer—together."

Dr. James Dobson, *What Wives Wish Their Husbands Knew about Women,* p. 186

This is what I have asked of God for you: that you will be encouraged and knit together by strong ties of love.
Colossians 2:2 TLB

OCTOBER 11

I am a firm believer in the judicious use of grace (and humor) in parent-child relationships.

Dr. James Dobson, *The New Dare to Discipline,* pp. 66–67

Bear with each other and forgive whatever grievances you may have against one another. Forgive as the Lord forgave you.

Colossians 3:13 NIV

MARCH 23

It does seem strange that we parents are so reluctant to share our adolescent experiences with our own children. Preteens could profit from what we have learned because we've been where they appear to be going.

Dr. James Dobson, *Preparing for Adolescence,* p. 11

Only fools refuse to be taught. Listen to your father and mother. What you learn from them will stand you in good stead; it will gain you many honors. Proverbs 1:8-9 TLB

OCTOBER 10

God is not a subservient genie who comes out of a bottle to sweep away each trial and hurdle which blocks our path. Rather, he offers us his will for *today* only. Our tomorrows must be met one day at a time, negotiated with a generous portion of faith.

Dr. James Dobson, *Dr. Dobson Answers Your Questions*, p. 486

So don't be anxious about tomorrow. God will take care of your tomorrow too. Live one day at a time.
Matthew 6:34 TLB

MARCH 24

Children of all ages seek constant satisfaction of their emotional needs, including the desire for love, social acceptance, and self-respect.

Dr. James Dobson, *The New Dare to Discipline*, p. 92

Satisfy us in the morning with your unfailing love, that we may sing for joy and be glad all our days.
Psalm 90:14 NIV

OCTOBER 9

I will make mistakes and errors as a parent. My human frailties are impossible to hide, and my children will occasionally fall victim to those imperfections. But I cannot abandon my responsibilities to provide leadership simply because I lack infinite wisdom and insight.

Dr. James Dobson, *Dr. Dobson Answers Your Questions about Raising Children*, p. 120

Don't worry about anything; instead, pray about everything; tell God your needs, and don't forget to thank him for his answers. If you do this, you will experience God's peace, which is far more wonderful than the human mind can understand.

Philippians 4:6-7 TLB

MARCH 25

Even when people genuinely love each other, there are times of great closeness, times when they feel nothing for each other, and times when they are irritable and grumpy. Emotions are like that. Therefore it is impossible for a married couple to maintain that peak of intensity with which their relationship began.

Dr. James Dobson, *Preparing for Adolescence,* p. 97

For I am convinced that neither death nor life, neither angels nor demons, neither the present nor the future . . . nor anything else in all creation, will be able to separate us from the love of God that is in Christ Jesus our Lord.
Romans 8:38-39 NIV

OCTOBER 8

If jealousy is so common, then how can parents minimize the natural antagonism that children feel for their siblings? The first step is to avoid circumstances that compare them unfavorably with each other.

Dr. James Dobson, *The Strong-Willed Child,* p. 128

Do for others what you want them to do for you. Matthew 7:12 TLB

$\mathcal{M}$ARCH 26

Much of the anger of today's youth is generated by their perception of injustice.

Dr. James Dobson, *Dr. Dobson Answers Your Questions,* p. 268

To do what is right and just is more acceptable to the Lord than sacrifice.
Proverbs 21:3 NIV

OCTOBER 7

Homework is valuable as an instrument of discipline.
Since adult life requires self-sacrifice, sweat, and devotion
to causes, school should help shape a child's capacity to
handle this future responsibility.

Dr. James Dobson, *The New Dare to Discipline,* pp. 194–195

*The sacrifices of God are a broken
spirit; a broken and contrite heart,
O God, you will not despise.*
Psalm 51:17 NIV

MARCH 27

"Routine panic" is becoming an American way of life.
Guess who is the inevitable loser from this breathless
life-style? It's the little guy who is leaning against the wall
with his hands in the pocket of his blue jeans.

Dr. James Dobson, *What Wives Wish Their Husbands Knew about Women*, p. 50

*Come, Lord, and show me your
mercy, for I am helpless,
overwhelmed, in deep distress; my
problems go from bad to worse.*
Psalm 25:16-17 TLB

OCTOBER 6

Change that which can be altered, explain that which can be learned, revise that which can be improved, resolve that which can be settled, and negotiate that which is open to compromise. Create the best marriage possible from the raw materials brought by two imperfect human beings with two distinctly unique personalities.

Dr. James Dobson, *What Wives Wish Their Husbands Knew about Women*, p. 183

You should be like one big happy family, full of sympathy toward each other, loving one another with tender hearts and humble minds.

1 Peter 3:8 TLB

MARCH 28

The overall objective during preadolescence is teaching the child that actions have inevitable consequences. One of the most serious casualties in a permissive society is the failure to connect those two factors: behavior and consequences.

Dr. James Dobson, *The New Dare to Discipline,* p. 116

I am he who searches hearts and minds, and I will repay each of you according to your deeds.
Revelation 2:23 NIV

CTOBER 5

Spanking a young child is much more effective if applied early in the conflict, while the parent's emotional apparatus is under control, than after ninety minutes of scratching and clawing.

Dr. James Dobson, *The Strong-Willed Child*, p. 36

There is a time for everything . . . a
time to be silent and a time to speak.
        Ecclesiastes 3:1, 7 NIV

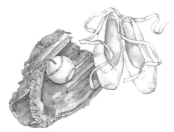

MARCH 29

Ultimately, the key to competent parenthood is being able to get behind the eyes of your child, seeing what he sees and feeling what he feels. When he is lonely, he needs your company. When he is defiant, he needs your help in controlling his impulses. . . . When he is happy, he needs to share his laughter and joy with those he loves.

Dr. James Dobson, *The Strong-Willed Child,* p. 121

Rejoice with those who rejoice; mourn with those who mourn.
Romans 12:15 NIV

OCTOBER 4

No longer is extreme violence something that happens only on television. It is a reality of daily life for many of our youth.

Dr. James Dobson, *The New Dare to Discipline*, p. 205

Let everyone call urgently on God.
Let them give up their evil ways and
their violence. Jonah 3:8 NIV

MARCH 30

While every child needs to be acquainted with denial of some of his more extravagant wishes, there is also a need for parents to consider each request on its own merit. There are so many necessary "no's" in life that we should say "yes" whenever we can.

Dr. James Dobson, *The Strong-Willed Child,* p. 115

For no matter how many promises God has made, they are "Yes" in Christ. 2 Corinthians 1:20 NIV

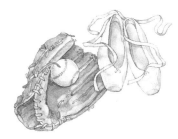

OCTOBER 3

No child should *ever* be allowed to make fun of another in a destructive way. Period! This should be an inflexible rule with no exceptions.

Dr. James Dobson, *The Strong-Willed Child,* p. 132

A true friend is always loyal, and a brother is born to help in time of need.
Proverbs 17:17 TLB

MARCH 31

Prescription for a happier, healthier life: resolve to slow your pace; learn to say no gracefully; resist the temptation to chase after more pleasures, hobbies, and social entanglements. You must "hold the line" . . . blocking out the intruders and defending the home team.

Dr. James Dobson, *What Wives Wish Their Husbands Knew about Women,* p. 54

*Better a dry crust with peace and
quiet than a house full of feasting,
with strife.* Proverbs 17:1 NIV

OCTOBER 2

I believe more divorces are caused by mutual overcommitment outside the home by husbands and wives than all other factors combined. It is the number one marriage killer!

Dr. James Dobson, *Dr. Dobson Answers Your Questions about Marriage and Sexuality*, p. 50

"Why has God abandoned us?" you cry. I'll tell you why; it is because the Lord has seen your treachery in divorcing your wives who have been faithful to you through the years, the companions you promised to care for and keep.   Malachi 2:14 TLB

APRIL 1

You don't have to spend a lot of money to preserve meaningful family life. Children love daily routine activities of the simplest kind. They enjoy hearing the same stories a thousand times over, and they'll laugh at the same jokes until you're ready to climb the wall from repeating them.

Dr. James Dobson, *Dr. Dobson Answers Your Questions*, p. 30

If you wait for perfect conditions, you will never get anything done.
Ecclesiastes 11:4 TLB

OCTOBER 1

There is no more ineffective method of controlling human beings (of all ages) than the use of irritation and anger.

Dr. James Dobson, *The Strong-Willed Child,* p. 99

A fool gives vent to his anger, but a wise man keeps himself under control.
Proverbs 29:11 NIV

 PRIL 2

We can make no greater mistake as a nation than to
continue this pervasive disrespect shown to women who
have devoted their lives to the welfare of their families.

Dr. James Dobson, *Dr. Dobson Answers Your Questions about Marriage and Sexuality,* p. 41

Treat . . . older women as mothers,
and younger women as sisters, with
absolute purity.   1 Timothy 5:1-2 NIV

SEPTEMBER 30

We should make it clear that the merciful God of love whom we serve is also a God of justice. An adolescent who understands this truth is more likely to live a moral life in the midst of an immoral society.

Dr. James Dobson, *The New Dare to Discipline,* p. 228

The LORD longs to be gracious to you; he rises to show you compassion. For the LORD is a God of justice. Blessed are all who wait for him!
Isaiah 30:18 NIV

APRIL 3

When you are tired you are attacked by ideas you thought you had conquered long ago.

Dr. James Dobson, *What Wives Wish Their Husbands Knew about Women*, p. 44

He was the one who prayed to the God of Israel, "Oh, that you would wonderfully bless me and help me in my work; please be with me in all that I do, and keep me from all evil and disaster!" And God granted him his request.   1 Chronicles 4:10 TLB

SEPTEMBER 29

Students can't learn without facing some hardships. And ultimately, an adolescent can't enter young adulthood until we release him from our protective custody.

Dr. James Dobson, *The Strong-Willed Child,* p. 218

It is possible to give away and become richer! It is also possible to hold on too tightly and lose everything.
Proverbs 11:24 TLB

APRIL 4

Be patient and give your child time to mature. Work gently on the traits that concern you the most, but allow him the privilege of being a child. He will be one for such a brief moment, anyway.

Dr. James Dobson, *Dr. Dobson Answers Your Questions about Raising Children,* p. 18

There is . . . a season for every activity under heaven.
Ecclesiastes 3:1 NIV

SEPTEMBER 28

Permissiveness has not just been a failure, it's been a disaster!

Dr. James Dobson, *Dare to Discipline*, p. 3

They were backbiters, haters of God, insolent, proud, braggarts, always thinking of new ways of sinning and continually being disobedient to their parents. They tried to misunderstand, broke their promises, and were heartless—without pity.
Romans 1:30-31 TLB

 PRIL 5

Everything worth having comes with a price. If improvement is to be made in the development of mental skills and knowledge, it will be accomplished through blood, sweat, and a few tears.

Dr. James Dobson, *The New Dare to Discipline,* p. 126.

You are not your own; you were bought at a price.
1 Corinthians 6:19-20 NIV

SEPTEMBER 27

It has been said that prosperity offers a greater test of character than does adversity. I am inclined to agree. There are few conditions that inhibit a sense of appreciation more than for a child to feel he is entitled to whatever he wants, whenever he wants it.

Dr. James Dobson, *Dare to Discipline,* p. 31

Watch out! Be on your guard against all kinds of greed; a man's life does not consist in the abundance of his possessions. Luke 12:15 NIV

APRIL 6

The three biggest sources of depression among American women: (1) "I don't like myself." (2) "I have no meaningful relationships outside my home." (3) "I am not even close to the man I love."

Dr. James Dobson, *What Wives Wish Their Husbands Knew about Women,* p. 59

I lie awake, lonely as a solitary sparrow on the roof. Psalm 102:7 TLB

SEPTEMBER 26

Success breeds success. The best motivation for a slow learner is to know he is succeeding. If adults in his life show confidence in him, he will more likely have confidence in himself. We tend to act the way we think other people "see" us.

Dr. James Dobson, *The New Dare to Discipline*, p. 177.

The LORD seeth not as man seeth;
for man looketh on the outward
appearance, but the LORD looketh
on the heart.   1 Samuel 16:7 KJV

APRIL 7

There's nothing wrong about feeling good about the successes of our children. The problem occurs when parents care too much about those triumphs and failures . . . when their own egos are riding on the kids' performances, when winning is necessary to maintain the parents' respect and love. Boys and girls should know they are accepted simply because they are God's own creation. That is enough!

Dr. James Dobson, *Dr. Dobson Answers Your Questions about Marriage and Sexuality,* p. 80

As it says in the Scriptures, "If anyone is going to boast, let him boast only of what the Lord has done."
1 Corinthians 1:31 TLB

$\mathscr{S}$EPTEMBER 25

Parents should be sensitive to the self-concept of their children, being especially mindful of matters pertaining to physical attractiveness or intelligence. These are two primary "soft spots" where boys and girls are most vulnerable.

Dr. James Dobson, *Dr. Dobson Answers Your Questions about Confident, Healthy Families*, p. 23

It is God himself who has made us what we are and given us new lives from Christ Jesus; and long ages ago he planned that we should spend these lives in helping others.
                    Ephesians 2:10 TLB

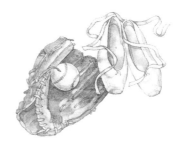

APRIL 8

A child should not be punished for behavior that is not willfully defiant. When he forgets to feed the dog or make his bed or take out the trash—when he leaves your tennis racket outside in the rain or loses his bicycle—remember that these behaviors are typical of childhood. Be gentle as you teach him to do better.

Dr. James Dobson, *The Strong-Willed Child*, p. 32

Let your gentleness be evident to all.
The Lord is near.   Philippians 4:5 NIV

SEPTEMBER 24

If it is desirable for children to be kind, appreciative, and pleasant, those qualities should be taught—not hoped for.

Dr. James Dobson, *The New Dare to Discipline,* pp. 14–15

A kindhearted woman gains respect, but ruthless men gain only wealth. A kind man benefits himself, but a cruel man brings trouble on himself.
Proverbs 11:16-17 NIV

 PRIL 9

Children are not casual guests in our home. They have
been loaned to us temporarily for the purpose of loving
them and instilling a foundation of values on which their
future lives will be built. We will be accountable through
eternity for the way we discharge that responsibility.

Dr. James Dobson, *The Strong-Willed Child,* p. 178

Train a child in the way he should go.
Proverbs 22:6 NIV

SEPTEMBER 23

Make no important, life-shaping decisions quickly or impulsively, and when in doubt, stall for time.

Dr. James Dobson, *What Wives Wish Their Husbands Knew about Women,* p. 93

Trust the Lord completely; don't ever trust yourself.   Proverbs 3:5 TLB

APRIL 10

Feelings of inadequacy, lack of confidence, and a certainty of worthlessness have become a way of life or, too often, a way of despair for millions of American women. It need not be so!

Dr. James Dobson, *What Wives Wish Their Husbands Knew about Women*, p. 22

Moreover, because of what Christ has done, we have become gifts to God that he delights in, for as part of God's sovereign plan we were chosen from the beginning to be his, and all things happen just as he decided long ago. Ephesians 1:11 TLB

SEPTEMBER 22

These principles represent the essence of my philosophy of discipline: (1) Define the boundaries before they are reinforced. (2) When defiantly challenged, respond with confident decisiveness. (3) Distinguish between willful defiance and childish irresponsibility. (4) Reassure and teach after the confrontation is over. (5) Avoid impossible demands. (6) Let love be your guide.

Dr. James Dobson, *Dr. Dobson Answers Your Questions about Raising Children,* pp. 127–128

Endure hardship as discipline; God is treating you as sons. For what son is not disciplined by his father?
Hebrews 12:7 NIV

 PRIL 11

The most vital responsibility in parenting—that of introducing our children to Jesus Christ and getting them safely through this dangerous and turbulent world—should be the ultimate goal for every believing parent the world over.

Dr. James Dobson, *The New Dare to Discipline,* p. 250

You must think constantly about these commandments I am giving you today. You must teach them to your children and talk about them when you are at home or out for a walk; at bedtime and the first thing in the morning. Deuteronomy 6:6-7 TLB

SEPTEMBER 21

The human brain is capable of storing two billion bits of data in a lifetime; education is the process of filling that memory bank with useful information and concepts. Most important, it should teach us how to think.

Dr. James Dobson, *The New Dare to Discipline*, p. 195

Do not conform any longer to the pattern of this world, but be transformed by the renewing of your mind. Romans 12:2 NIV

 PRIL 12

The husband must recognize the wife's feelings and needs as being one with his own. When she hurts, he hurts, and takes steps to end the pain. What she needs, he needs, and tries to satisfy. . . . If this one prescription were applied . . . we would have little need for divorce courts.

Dr. James Dobson, *What Wives Wish Their Husbands Knew about Women,* p. 70

Husbands ought to love their wives as their own bodies. He who loves his wife loves himself. After all, no one ever hated his own body, but he feeds and cares for it, just as Christ does the church. Ephesians 5:28-30 NIV

SEPTEMBER 20

If a man wants his wife to accept the responsibility of motherhood and all that it implies, then he must provide her with his support and involvement. . . . He must help her discipline, train, and guide; he must meet her emotional and romantic needs which accumulate in his absence; . . . and most important, he must reserve some of his time for his family.

Dr. James Dobson, *What Wives Wish Their Husbands Knew about Women,* p. 162

But remember that in God's plan men and women need each other.
    1 Corinthians 11:11 TLB

APRIL 13

Don't struggle with things you can't change. The first principle of mental health is to learn to accept the inevitable. To do otherwise is to run with the brakes on. Too many people make themselves unhappy over insignificant irritants which should be ignored.

Dr. James Dobson, *The New Dare to Discipline,* p. 246

In repentance and rest is your salvation, in quietness and trust is your strength. Isaiah 30:15 NIV

SEPTEMBER 19

Children are expensive, but they're worth the price.
Besides, nothing worth having comes cheap.

Dr. James Dobson, *Dr. Dobson Answers Your Questions about Raising Children,* p. 32

*Children are a gift from God; they are
his reward.* Psalm 127:3 TLB

 # APRIL 14

In matters relative to beauty, brains, and athletic ability, each child should know that in his parents' eyes, he is respected and has equal worth with his siblings. Praise and criticism at home should be distributed as evenly as possible.

Dr. James Dobson, *The Strong-Willed Child*, p. 130

God does not show favoritism.
Acts 10:34 NIV

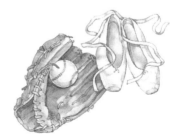

$\mathcal{S}$EPTEMBER 18

Most confusion over how to discipline results from
parents' failure to define the limits properly.

Dr. James Dobson, *The Strong-Willed Child*, p. 71

King Solomon . . . wrote [the
proverbs] to teach his people how
to live—how to act in every
circumstance.   Proverbs 1:1-2 TLB

 PRIL 15

All problems seem more unsolvable at night, and the decisions that are reached then may be more emotional than rational. A good night's sleep and a rich cup of coffee can go a long way toward defusing the problem.

Dr. James Dobson, *Dare to Discipline*, p. 194

Let me see your kindness to me in the morning, for I am trusting you. Show me where to walk, for my prayer is sincere. Psalm 143:8 TLB

SEPTEMBER 17

Citizenship Day

If it is important to produce respectful, responsible young citizens, then we should set out to mold them accordingly.

Dr. James Dobson, *The New Dare to Discipline*, p. 15

But our citizenship is in heaven. And we eagerly await a Savior from there, the Lord Jesus Christ.
Philippians 3:20 NIV

 PRIL 16

We are not typically kind and loving and generous and yielded to God. Our tendency is toward selfishness and stubbornness and sin. We are all, in effect, "strong-willed children" as we stand before God.

Dr. James Dobson, *The Strong-Willed Child*, pp. 174–175

He passed in front of Moses, proclaiming, "The LORD, the LORD, the compassionate and gracious God, slow to anger, abounding in love and faithfulness, maintaining love to thousands, and forgiving wickedness, rebellion and sin."

Exodus 34:6-7 NIV

SEPTEMBER 16

The task of forming healthy sexual attitudes and understandings in children requires considerable skill and tact. For those parents who are able to handle the instructional process correctly, the responsibility should be retained in the home.

Dr. James Dobson, *The New Dare to Discipline,* p. 217

Let us turn away from everything
wrong, whether of body or spirit . . .
giving ourselves to him alone.
2 Corinthians 7:1 TLB

APRIL 17

The parent must convince himself that discipline is not something he does *to* the child; it is something he does *for* the child.

Dr. James Dobson, *Dare to Discipline*, p. 18

He who spares the rod hates his son, but he who loves him is careful to discipline him.   Proverbs 13:24 NIV

SEPTEMBER 15

We all have human worth, yet so many young people conclude that they're somehow different—that they're truly inferior—that they lack the necessary ingredients for dignity and worth.

Dr. James Dobson, *Preparing for Adolescence*, p. 18

For you created my inmost being; you knit me together in my mother's womb. I praise you because I am fearfully and wonderfully made; your works are wonderful, I know that full well. Psalm 139:13-14 NIV

APRIL 18

The hand is an object of love and should not be used as an instrument of corporal punishment. If all spankings are administered with a neutral object, applied where intended, then the child need never fear that he will suddenly be chastised for some accidental indiscretion when the parent makes a sudden move.

Dr. James Dobson, *The Strong-Willed Child,* p. 46

Sometimes mere words are not enough—discipline is needed. For the words may not be heeded.
Proverbs 29:19 TLB

SEPTEMBER 14

Creativity can flourish only when there's enough order in the classroom to allow for concentrated thought. Chaos and creativity don't mix.

Dr. James Dobson, *The New Dare to Discipline,* p. 151

Be still, and know that I am God.
                Psalm 46:10 NIV

APRIL 19

Don't argue with your teen. Don't subject him to perpetual threats and finger-wagging accusations and insulting indictments. And most important, don't nag him endlessly.

Dr. James Dobson, *The Strong-Willed Child*, p. 202

Don't have anything to do with foolish and stupid arguments, because you know they produce quarrels. And the Lord's servant must not quarrel. 2 Timothy 2:23-24 NIV

SEPTEMBER 13

Moms and dads, your highest priority is to lead your children into the fold. Don't stop praying until that objective is fulfilled.

Dr. James Dobson, *When God Doesn't Make Sense,* p. 207

Fix these words of mine in your hearts and minds. . . . Teach them to your children, talking about them when you sit at home and when you walk along the road, when you lie down and when you get up.
Deuteronomy 11:18-19 NIV

APRIL 20

If it is desirable that children be kind, appreciative, and pleasant, those qualities should be taught—not hoped for. Heredity does not equip a child with proper attitudes; children will learn what they are taught.

Dr. James Dobson, *Dare to Discipline,* p. 9

He has showed you, O man, what is good. And what does the Lord require of you? To act justly and to love mercy and to walk humbly with your God. Micah 6:8 NIV

SEPTEMBER 12

Healthy parenthood can be boiled down to those two
essential ingredients, love and control, operating in a
system of checks and balances.

Dr. James Dobson, *The Strong-Willed Child,* p. 52

Therefore encourage one another and
build each other up.
         1 Thessalonians 5:11 NIV

APRIL 21

Parents should always watch for opportunities to offer genuine, well-deserved praise to their children, while avoiding empty flattery.

Dr. James Dobson, *The New Dare to Discipline*, p. 96

Whatever is true, whatever is noble, whatever is right, whatever is pure, whatever is lovely, whatever is admirable—if anything is excellent or praiseworthy—think about such things. Philippians 4:8 NIV

SEPTEMBER 11

Play is important in a child's life. Youngsters should not work all the time. The home and school should provide a healthy balance between discipline and play.

Dr. James Dobson, *The New Dare to Discipline,* p. 195

Let them praise his name with
dancing and make music to him with
tambourine and harp. For the LORD
takes delight in his people; he crowns
the humble with salvation.
Psalm 149:3-4 NIV

APRIL 22

Many (if not most) marriages suffer from a failure to recognize a universal characteristic of human nature. *We value that which we are fortunate to get; we discredit that with which we are stuck!*

Dr. James Dobson, *What Wives Wish Their Husbands Knew about Women*, p. 78

Keep faith with the wife of your youth.
Malachi 2:15 TLB

SEPTEMBER 10

Grandmothers and grandfathers can be invaluable to the world of little people. For one thing, "They are the only grown-ups who have time."

Dr. James Dobson, *What Wives Wish Their Husbands Knew about Women,* p. 49

Children's children are a crown to the aged, and parents are the pride of their children. Proverbs 17:6 NIV

APRIL 23

Undeserved guilt is one of the most powerful weapons in the devil's arsenal. By seeming to ally himself with the voice of the Holy Spirit, Satan uses the conscience to accuse, torment, and berate his victims. What better tool for spiritual discouragement could there be than feelings of guilt which cannot be "forgiven"—because they do not represent genuine disapproval from God?

Dr. James Dobson, *Dr. Dobson Answers Your Questions about Confident, Healthy Families*, p. 116

But now [Christ] has appeared once for all at the end of the ages to do away with sin by the sacrifice of himself. Hebrews 9:26 NIV

SEPTEMBER 9

Teachers who maintain order without being angry are often the most respected. There is safety in order, and children love secure environments.

Dr. James Dobson, *Dare to Discipline,* p. 106

A wise teacher makes learning a joy.
Proverbs 15:2 TLB

APRIL 24

Suppose the parents of yesterday could visit our time to observe the conditions that prevail among our children. They would be appalled by the problems that have become widespread in our homes, schools, and neighborhoods.

Dr. James Dobson, *The New Dare to Discipline,* p. 203

But we are all as an unclean thing, and all our righteousnesses are as filthy rags; and we all do fade as a leaf; and our iniquities, like the wind, have taken us away. Isaiah 64:6 KJV

SEPTEMBER 8

Can you accept the fact that your mate will never be able to meet all your needs and aspirations? Seldom does one human being satisfy every longing and hope in another. Both partners have to settle for human foibles and faults and irritability and fatigue and occasional nighttime "headaches."

Dr. James Dobson, *What Wives Wish Their Husbands Knew About Women*, p. 65

For God is at work within you,
helping you want to obey him, and
then helping you do what he wants.
Philippians 2:13 TLB

 PRIL 25

All believers will "run aground" at some point in their lives, and they (we) must learn not to panic when the ship grinds into a sandbar! That poise under pressure *can* be learned to some degree.

Dr. James Dobson, *When God Doesn't Make Sense,* pp. 106–107

Those who trust in the Lord are steady as Mount Zion, unmoved by any circumstance. Psalm 125:1 TLB

$\mathscr{S}$EPTEMBER 7

Regarding the timing of sex education in the home, parents should plan to end their instructional program immediately before their child enters puberty. Once they enter this developmental period, they are typically embarrassed by discussions of sex with their parents. We should respect this. We are given ten to twelve years to provide the proper understanding of human sexuality; after that . . . we can only serve as resources.

Dr. James Dobson, *Dare to Discipline,* p. 152

I have thought much about your words and stored them in my heart so that they would hold me back from sin.
Psalm 119:11 TLB

APRIL 26

When a parent refuses to accept his child's defiant challenge, something changes in their relationship. The youngster begins to look at his mother and father with disrespect; they are unworthy of his allegiance.

Dr. James Dobson, *The Strong-Willed Child,* p. 18

He must . . . see that his children
obey him with proper respect.
1 Timothy 3:4 NIV

SEPTEMBER 6

Provide your children with many interesting books and materials, read to them and answer their questions.

Dr. James Dobson, *The New Dare to Discipline,* p. 181

May God be with you. You must be the people's representative before God. . . . Teach them the decrees and laws, and show them the way to live.
Exodus 18:19-20 NIV

APRIL 27

It is imperative that parents take the time and invest their resources in their children. The necessity for providing rich, edifying experiences for young children has never been so pressing as it is today.

Dr. James Dobson, *The New Dare to Discipline,* p. 181

If you then, though you are evil, know how to give good gifts to your children, how much more will your Father in heaven give the Holy Spirit to those who ask him!

Luke 11:13 NIV

SEPTEMBER 5

Parents who recognize the inevitable internal war between good and evil will do their best to influence the child's choices—to shape his will and provide a solid spiritual foundation.

Dr. James Dobson, *Dr. Dobson Answers Your Questions,* p. 44

We know that we are children of God and that all the rest of the world around us is under Satan's power and control. 1 John 5:19 TLB

 PRIL 28

Committed love is expensive, but it yields the highest returns on the investment at maturity.

Dr. James Dobson, *What Wives Wish Their Husbands Knew about Women*, p. 176

If you love someone, you will be loyal to him no matter what the cost. You will always believe in him, always expect the best of him, and always stand your ground in defending him.
1 Corinthians 13:7 TLB

SEPTEMBER 4

If I can lead but one lost human being to the personhood of Jesus Christ—the giver of life itself—then I need no other justification for my earthly existence.

Dr. James Dobson, *Dr. Dobson Answers Your Questions about Confident, Healthy Families,* p. 11

I try to please everyone in everything I do, not doing what I like or what is best for me but what is best for them, so that they may be saved.
1 Corinthians 10:33 TLB

APRIL 29

Their respect for strength and courage makes children want to know how "tough" their leaders are. They will occasionally disobey parental instructions for the precise purpose of testing the determination of those in charge.

Dr. James Dobson, *The Strong-Willed Child,* p. 16

Obey your leaders and submit to
their authority. They keep watch over
you as men who must give an
account.   Hebrews 13:17 NIV

SEPTEMBER 3

Our children are not casual guests in our home. They have been loaned to us temporarily for the purpose of loving them and instilling a foundation of values on which their future lives will be built. And we will be accountable through eternity for the way we discharged that responsibility.

Dr. James Dobson, *Dr. Dobson Answers Your Questions about Raising Children*, p. 118

I asked him to give me this child, and
he has given me my request; and now
I am giving him to the Lord for as
long as he lives.

1 Samuel 1:27-28 TLB

APRIL 30

One of the primary responsibilities of parents and teachers is to teach children to love one another. It can be done. Most boys and girls have a tender spirit beneath the unsympathetic exterior.

Dr. James Dobson, *Dr. Dobson Answers Your Questions,* p. 500

Let us practice loving each other, for love comes from God and those who are loving and kind show that they are the children of God, and that they are getting to know him better.
1 John 4:7 TLB

SEPTEMBER 2

It is my guess that 90 percent of divorces involve an extremely busy husband who is in love with his work and who tends to be somewhat insensitive, unromantic, and noncommunicative, married to a lonely, vulnerable, romantic woman who has severe doubts about her worth.

Dr. James Dobson, *Dr. Dobson Answers Your Questions,* p. 335

Husbands, show the same kind of love to your wives as Christ showed to the Church when he died for her.
Ephesians 5:25 TLB

$\mathcal{M}$AY 1

Parents should guard against comparative statements which routinely favor one child over another. This is particularly true in three areas: physical attractiveness, intelligence, and athletic abilities.

Dr. James Dobson, *The Strong-Willed Child*, pp. 128–129

O Lord, you are our Father. We are the clay, you are the potter; we are all the work of your hand.

Isaiah 64:8 NIV

SEPTEMBER 1

Children are very concerned about the threat of being laughed at by their friends and will sometimes go to great lengths to avoid that possibility. Conformity is fueled by the fear of ridicule. Teens, particularly, seem to feel, "The group can't laugh at me if I am identical to them."

Dr. James Dobson, *The New Dare to Discipline*, pp. 181–182

Do not love the world or anything in the world. . . . The world and its desires pass away, but the man who does the will of God lives forever.
1 John 2:15, 17 NIV

MAY 2

Learning is important because we are changed by what we learn, even if the facts are later forgotten. Learning changes values, attitudes, and concepts that don't fade in time.

Dr. James Dobson, *The New Dare to Discipline*, p. 195

And we, who with unveiled faces all reflect the Lord's glory, are being transformed into his likeness with ever-increasing glory, which comes from the Lord, who is the Spirit.
2 Corinthians 3:18 NIV

AUGUST 31

When the family conforms to God's blueprint . . . the chain has no weak links. It reveals the beauty of God's own creation, as does the rest of his universe.

Dr. James Dobson, *What Wives Wish Their Husbands Knew about Women,* pp. 185–186

The reverence and fear of God are basic to all wisdom. Knowing God results in every other kind of understanding. "I, Wisdom, will make the hours of your day more profitable and the years of your life more fruitful." Proverbs 9:10-11 TLB

MAY 3

The most frustrating aspect of the "terrible twos" is the tendency of kids to spill things, destroy things, eat horrible things, fall off of things, kill things, and get into things. They also have a knack for doing embarrassing things, like sneezing on a man at the lunch counter. During these toddler years, any unexplained silence of more than thirty seconds can throw an adult into sudden panic.

Dr. James Dobson, *The Strong-Willed Child,* p. 50

And he took the children in his arms, put his hands on them and blessed them. Mark 10:16 NIV

AUGUST 30

What does a woman most want from her husband in the fifth, sixth, and seventh decades of her life? She wants and needs the same assurance of love and respect that she desired when she was younger.

Dr. James Dobson, *What Wives Wish Their Husbands Knew about Women,* p. 176

If you can find a truly good wife, she is worth more than precious gems!
Proverbs 31:10 TLB

$\mathcal{M}$AY 4

The reason the average woman would rather have beauty than brains is because she knows that the average man can see better than he can think (no offense intended, gentlemen).

Dr. James Dobson, *What Wives Wish Their Husbands Knew about Women,* p. 28

*Be beautiful inside, in your hearts,
with the lasting charm of a gentle and
quiet spirit that is so precious to God.*
1 Peter 3:4 TLB

AUGUST 29

Every child is of equal worth in the sight of God.

Dr. James Dobson, *The New Dare to Discipline*, p. 199

*But Jesus called them unto him, and
said, Suffer little children to come
unto me, and forbid them not: for of
such is the kingdom of God.*

Luke 18:16 KJV

MAY 5

Establish reasonable expectations and boundaries in advance. The child should know what is and what is not acceptable behavior before he is held responsible for those rules. If you haven't defined it—don't enforce it!

Dr. James Dobson, *The Strong-Willed Child,* p. 31

Point out anything you find in me that makes you sad, and lead me along the path of everlasting life.
Psalm 139:24 TLB

There is a narrow difference between acceptable, healthy "awe" and destructive fear. A child should have a general apprehension about the consequences of defying his parents. By contrast, he should not lie awake at night worrying about parental harshness or hostility.

Dr. James Dobson, *Dr. Dobson Answers Your Questions about Raising Children,* p. 135

He who fears the LORD has a secure fortress, and for his children it will be a refuge. Proverbs 14:26 NIV

$\mathscr{M}$AY 6

After a time of conflict it is extremely important to pray
with the child, admitting to God that we have all sinned
and no one is perfect. Divine forgiveness is a marvelous
experience, even for a very young child.

Dr. James Dobson, *The Strong-Willed Child*, p. 33

*If we confess our sins, he is faithful
and just to forgive us our sins, and to
cleanse us from all unrighteousness.*
1 John 1:9 KJV

AUGUST 27

Each child's room should be his private territory if space permits. Families with more than one child in each bedroom can allocate available living space for each youngster.

Dr. James Dobson, *The Strong-Willed Child*, p. 132

If it is possible, as far as it depends on you, live at peace with everyone.
Romans 12:18 NIV

Although love is essential to human life, parental responsibility extends far beyond it. . . . Love in the absence of instruction will not produce a child with self-discipline, self-control, and respect for his fellow man. Affection and warmth underlie all mental and physical health, yet they do not eliminate the need for careful training and guidance. **Dr. James Dobson**, *Dare to Discipline*, p. 10

"Adonijah has become king, and you, my lord the king, do not know about it." . . . (His father had never interfered with him by asking, "Why do you behave as you do?")
1 Kings 1:18, 6 NIV

AUGUST 26

Children of an appropriate age should be allowed to select their own clothes, within certain limits of the budget and good taste.

Dr. James Dobson, *The New Dare to Discipline,* p. 182

See how the lilies of the field grow. They do not labor or spin. Yet I tell you that not even Solomon in all his splendor was dressed like one of these. If that is how God clothes the grass of the field . . . will he not much more clothe you?

Matthew 6:28-30 NIV

MAY 8

To the exhausted and harassed new mother, let me say,
"Hang tough!" You are doing the most important job in
the universe!

Dr. James Dobson, *The Strong-Willed Child*, p. 40

*Trust and reverence the Lord . . . then
you will be given renewed health and
vitality.* Proverbs 3:7-8 TLB

$\mathscr{A}$UGUST 25

Self-esteem is generated by what we see in the eyes of other people. It is only when others respect us that we respect ourselves. It is only when others love us that we love ourselves. It is only when others find us pleasant and desirable and worthy that we come to terms with our own needs. God made us vulnerable to each other in this way.

Dr. James Dobson, *What Wives Wish Their Husbands Knew about Women,* p. 60

*Woe to those who are wise and
shrewd in their own eyes!*
            Isaiah 5:21 TLB

MAY 9

I have developed a great appreciation for the unique skills
required of wives and mothers. In my view, their job is
of utmost importance to the health and vitality of any
society, and I regret the lack of respect and status given
to today's homemaker.

Dr. James Dobson, *What Wives Wish Their Husbands Knew about Women,* p. 12

*Hold them in the highest regard in
love because of their work. Live in
peace with each other.*
1 Thessalonians 5:13 NIV

$\mathcal{A}$UGUST 24

Verbal reinforcement should permeate the entire parent-child relationship. Too often our parental instruction consists of a million "don'ts." We should spend more time rewarding him for the behavior we desire, even if our "reward" is nothing more than a sincere compliment.

Dr. James Dobson, *The New Dare to Discipline*, p. 94

A word aptly spoken is like apples of gold in settings of silver.
Proverbs 25:11 NIV

MAY 10

Being a good mother is one of the most complex skills in life. What activity could be more important than shaping human lives during their impressionable and plastic years?

Dr. James Dobson, *Dare to Discipline*, p. 40

Her children stand and bless her; so does her husband. He praises her with these words: "There are many fine women in the world, but you are the best of them all!"
Proverbs 31:28-29 TLB

AUGUST 23

What greater ego satisfaction could there be [for a child] than knowing that the Creator of the universe is acquainted with me, personally? That he understands my fears and anxieties; that his only Son, Jesus, gave his life for me; that he can turn my liabilities into assets and my emptiness into fullness; that a better life follows this one! This is fulfillment at its richest!

Dr. James Dobson, *Dr. Dobson Answers Your Questions about Confident, Healthy Families,* p. 26

I will be your God through all your lifetime, yes, even when your hair is white with age. I made you and I will care for you. Isaiah 46:4 TLB

MAY 11

Children are terribly dependent on their parents, and the task of meeting their needs is a full-time job.

Dr. James Dobson, *The New Dare to Discipline*, p. 243

Whatever you do, work at it with all your heart, as working for the Lord, not for men, since you know that you will receive an inheritance from the Lord as a reward.

Colossians 3:23-24 NIV

AUGUST 22

It is important for men to be able (and willing) to cry and love and hope. . . . Both men and women must learn to ventilate their feelings and be "real" people, without yielding to the tyranny of fluctuating emotions.

Dr. James Dobson, *Dr. Dobson Answers Your Questions about Marriage and Sexuality,* p. 77

Your affections . . . influence
everything else in your life.
                    Proverbs 4:23 TLB

MAY 12

Kids love games of all sorts, especially if adults will get involved with them. It is often possible to turn a teaching situation into a fun activity which "sensitizes" the entire family to the issue you're trying to teach.

Dr. James Dobson, *The Strong-Willed Child,* p. 163

Whatever a person is like, I try to find common ground with him.
1 Corinthians 9:22 TLB

AUGUST 21

A husband and wife should have a date every week or two, leaving the children at home and forgetting the day's problems for an evening.

Dr. James Dobson, *The New Dare to Discipline,* p. 245

He who finds a wife finds what is good and receives favor from the LORD. Proverbs 18:22 NIV

$\mathcal{M}$AY 13

Being a mother or father is not only one of life's greatest joys, but it can also represent a personal sacrifice and challenge. Everything of value is expensive, and children are no exception to the rule.

Dr. James Dobson, *The Strong-Willed Child*, p. 126

The father of a righteous man has great joy; he who has a wise son delights in him. Proverbs 23:24 NIV

AUGUST 20

Unless a woman feels a certain closeness to her husband—unless she believes he respects her—she may be unable to enjoy a sexual encounter with him.

Dr. James Dobson, *What Wives Wish Their Husbands Knew about Women*, p. 116

I appeal to you, brothers, in the name of our Lord Jesus Christ, that all of you agree with one another so that there may be no divisions among you and that you may be perfectly united in mind and thought.
1 Corinthians 1:10 NIV

MAY 14

It is imperative that a child learns to respect his parents—not to satisfy their egos, but because his relationship with them provides the basis for his later attitude toward all other people.

Dr. James Dobson, *The New Dare to Discipline,* p. 18

Honor your father and your mother, as the LORD your God has commanded you, so that you may live long and that it may go well with you in the land the LORD your God is giving you. Deuteronomy 5:16 NIV

AUGUST 19

The goal of proper child rearing is not to produce perfect kids. Even if you implement a flawless system of discipline at home, which no one in history has done, your children will be children.

Dr. James Dobson, *The New Dare to Discipline*, p. 34

Like arrows in the hands of a warrior are sons born in one's youth. Blessed is the man whose quiver is full of them. Psalm 127:4-5 NIV

$\mathscr{M}$AY 15

I wonder how many times I have asked God to open the door on my "cage," not appreciating the security it was providing. I resolve to accept his negative answers with greater submission in the future.

Dr. James Dobson, *Dr. Dobson Answers Your Questions about Raising Children*, p. 121

Be joyful in hope, patient in affliction, faithful in prayer.

Romans 12:12 NIV

AUGUST 18

Within the human family, only one conclusion can be
drawn: God will do what is best, and we must continue to
trust Him regardless of the outcome.

Dr. James Dobson, *When God Doesn't Make Sense*, pp. 119–120

I am depending on you, O Lord my
God. Psalm 7:1 TLB

ℳAY 16

The ultimate paradox of childhood is that boys and girls
want to be led by their parents, but they insist that their
mothers and fathers earn the right to lead them.

Dr. James Dobson, *The Strong-Willed Child*, p. 18

*Teach me your way, O LORD; lead me
in a straight path.*   Psalm 27:11 NIV

$\mathcal{A}$UGUST 17

Parents of compliant children don't understand their friends with defiant youngsters. They intensify guilt and anxiety by implying, "If you would raise your kids the way I do it, you wouldn't be having those problems." . . . The willful child can be difficult to handle even when his parents lead him with great skill and dedication.

Dr. James Dobson, *Dr. Dobson Answers Your Questions about Raising Children,* p. 100

Ability to give wise advice satisfies like a good meal!

Proverbs 18:20 TLB

MAY 17

Permissiveness has not simply failed as an approach to child rearing. It's been a disaster for those who have tried it.

Dr. James Dobson, *The New Dare to Discipline*, p. 7

A child left to himself disgraces his mother. Proverbs 29:15 NIV

AUGUST 16

Reserve some time for yourself. It is unhealthy for anyone to work all the time.

Dr. James Dobson, *The New Dare to Discipline,* p. 245

My soul finds rest in God alone; my salvation comes from him.
Psalm 62:1 NIV

$\mathcal{M}$AY 18

Sensitivity to the feelings of the teen is paramount. If he or she wishes to talk, by all means, welcome the conversation. In other cases, parental guidance may be most effective if offered indirectly.

Dr. James Dobson, *The New Dare to Discipline*, p: 225

Listen, my son, accept what I say, and the years of your life will be many. I guide you in the way of wisdom and lead you along straight paths.
Proverbs 4:10-11 NIV

AUGUST 15

The Lord emphasizes in his Word that each of us is worth more than the possessions of the entire world. This is true just because we are human beings—not because of the way we look, or to whom we are married, or what our parents do, or how much money we have, or how much we have accomplished in life. Those earthly factors make no difference to God.

Dr. James Dobson, *Preparing for Adolescence,* p. 38

God knoweth your hearts: for that which is highly esteemed among men is abomination in the sight of God.
Luke 16:15 KJV

$\mathcal{M}$AY 19

Love is not defined by the highs and lows, but is
dependent on a commitment of the will.

Dr. James Dobson, *What Wives Wish Their Husbands Knew about Women*, p. 91

*Let us not love with words or tongue
but with actions and in truth.*
                    1 John 3:18 NIV

AUGUST 14

.One of the most important responsibilities in the Christian life is to care about other people—to smile at them and to be a friend of the friendless. God wants to use you to help his other children.

Dr. James Dobson, *Preparing for Adolescence,* p. 37

The King will reply, "I tell you the truth, whatever you did for one of the least of these brothers of mine, you did for me." Matthew 25:40 NIV

$\mathcal{M}$AY 20

[Emotions] are manipulated by hormones—especially in the teen years—and they wobble dramatically from early morning, when we're rested, to the evening, when we're tired. One of the evidences of emotional maturity is the ability (and the willingness) to overrule ephemeral feelings and govern our behavior with the intellect and the will. **Dr. James Dobson,** *When God Doesn't Make Sense,* p. 47

Perseverance must finish its work so that you may be mature and complete, not lacking anything.
James 1:4 NIV

AUGUST 13

Heredity does not equip a child with proper attitudes; children learn what they are taught. We cannot expect the coveted behavior to appear magically.

Dr. James Dobson, *The New Dare to Discipline*, p. 15

You were taught, with regard to your former way of life, to put off your old self . . . to be made new in the attitude of your minds; and to put on the new self, created to be like God in true righteousness and holiness.
Ephesians 4:22-24 NIV

$\mathcal{M}$AY 21

Children are incredibly vulnerable to rejection, ridicule, criticism, and anger at home, and they deserve to grow up in an environment of safety, acceptance, and warmth.

Dr. James Dobson, *The New Dare to Discipline*, pp. 12–13

Accept one another, then, just as
Christ accepted you, in order to bring
praise to God. Romans 15:7 NIV

AUGUST 12

We human beings can survive the most difficult of circumstances if we are not forced to stand alone. We are social creatures and can no better tolerate emotional solitude than Adam did before Eve was offered as his companion. Women need men, and men need women, and that's the way it has always been.

Dr. James Dobson, *What Wives Wish Their Husbands Knew about Women,* p. 185

If two lie down together, they will keep warm. But how can one keep warm alone? Though one may be overpowered, two can defend themselves. A cord of three strands is not quickly broken.

Ecclesiastes 4:11-12 NIV

MAY 22

Honesty which does not have the best interest of the
hearer at heart is a cruel form of selfishness.

Dr. James Dobson, *What Wives Wish Their Husbands Knew about Women*, p. 41

Don't be too eager to tell others their
faults, for we all make many
mistakes. James 3:1 TLB

AUGUST 11

One of your most important responsibilities is to establish an equitable system of justice and a balance of power between siblings at home.

Dr. James Dobson, *The Strong-Willed Child*, p. 132

The Lord loves justice and fairness.
Psalm 37:28 TLB

MAY 23

We learn from adversity. The parent who is too anxious to bail his child out of difficulty may be doing him a disservice.

Dr. James Dobson, *Dare to Discipline,* p. 103

When he came to his senses he said, ". . . I will set out and go back to my father and say to him: Father, I have sinned against heaven and against you." Luke 15:17-18 NIV

AUGUST 10

Parents who are cold and stern with their sons and daughters often leave them damaged for life. I don't believe in parental harshness.

Dr. James Dobson, *The New Dare to Discipline*, p. 12

Be completely humble and gentle; be patient, bearing with one another in love. Ephesians 4:2 NIV

MAY 24

Children need to be taught self-discipline and responsible behavior. They need assistance in learning how to handle the challenges and obligations of living. They must learn the art of self-control.

Dr. James Dobson, *The New Dare to Discipline,* p. 6

Like a city whose walls are broken down is a man who lacks self-control.
Proverbs 25:28 NIV

Did you know that God sees you when you hurt? He knows those deep fears and frustrations that you thought no one understood. He knows the longings of your heart.

Dr. James Dobson, *Preparing for Adolescence,* p. 33

O LORD, you have searched me and you know me. You know when I sit and when I rise; you perceive my thoughts from afar. You discern my going out and my lying down; you are familiar with all my ways.

Psalm 139:1-3 NIV

$\mathscr{M}$AY 25

The success of my relationship with my wife, Shirley, does not come from perfection of either my part or hers. It is simply a product of caring for feelings, needs, and concerns of the other. It is giving, not grabbing. And by some strange quirk of human nature, that attitude produces self-esteem by the bushel.

Dr. James Dobson, *What Wives Wish Their Husbands Knew about Women,* p. 72

Love does no wrong to anyone. That's why it fully satisfies all of God's requirements. It is the only law you need. Romans 13:10 TLB

$\mathscr{A}$UGUST 8

Should a spanking (age ten or less) hurt? Yes, or else it will have no influence. A swat on the behind through three layers of wet diapers simply conveys no urgent message. However, a small amount of pain for a young child goes a long way; it is certainly not necessary to be harsh or oppressive with him.

Dr. James Dobson, *The Strong-Willed Child,* p. 47

If you punish [your child] with the rod, he will not die. Punish him with the rod and save his soul from death.
Proverbs 23:13-14 NIV

$\mathcal{M}$AY 26

Sincere, dedicated believers go through tunnels and storms, too. We inflict a tremendous disservice on young Christians by making them think only sinners experience confusion and depressing times in their lives.

Dr. James Dobson, *Dr. Dobson Answers Your Questions,* p. 485

These trials are only to test your faith, to see whether or not it is strong and pure.   1 Peter 1:7 TLB

I recommend a simple principle: when you are defiantly challenged, win decisively. When the child asks, "Who's in charge?" tell him. When he mutters, "Who loves me?" take him in your arms and surround him with affection. Treat him with respect and dignity, and expect the same from him.

Dr. James Dobson, *The New Dare to Discipline*, p. 51

Discipline your son and he will give you happiness and peace of mind.
                    Proverbs 29:17 TLB

$\mathcal{M}$AY 27

The most effective parents are those who have the skill to get behind the eyes of their child, seeing what he sees, thinking what he thinks, feeling what he feels. The art of good parenthood revolves around the interpretation of meaning behind behavior.

Dr. James Dobson, *The New Dare to Discipline,* p. 29

Know thou the God of thy father, and serve him with a perfect heart and with a willing mind: for the Lord searcheth all hearts, and understandeth all the imaginations of the thoughts.

1 Chronicles 28:9 KJV

AUGUST 6

Children need adults who can go for casual walks and talk about fishing, to look at pretty leaves and caterpillars . . . and answer questions about God and the nature of the world as it is.

Dr. James Dobson, *What Wives Wish Their Husbands Knew about Women*, p. 49

The Lord who gives us sunlight in the daytime and the moon and stars to light the night, and who stirs the sea to make the roaring waves—his name is Lord Almighty.

Jeremiah 31:35 TLB

MAY 28

It is most important that a child respect his parents because the child's relationship with his parents provides the basis for his attitude toward all other people.

Dr. James Dobson, *Dare to Discipline,* p. 14

Obey those over you, and give honor and respect to all those to whom it is due. Romans 13:7 TLB

AUGUST 5

I am very concerned by the number of mothers of *preschool* children holding down full-time employment in situations which do not require it. This abandonment of the home may be our gravest and most dangerous mistake as a nation!

Dr. James Dobson, *What Wives Wish Their Husbands Knew about Women*, p. 55

Realize that you must account to God for everything you do.
Ecclesiastes 11:9 TLB

MAY 29

Some young adults who have grown up in an atmosphere of love and discipline in balance are now raising their children that way.

Dr. James Dobson, *The New Dare to Discipline*, p. 244

For I have chosen him, so that he will direct his children and his household after him to keep the way of the LORD by doing what is right and just.
Genesis 18:19 NIV

The happiest people in the world are not those who have no problems, but the people who have learned to live with those things that are less than perfect.

Dr. James Dobson, *Preparing for Adolescence,* p. 32

But he said to me, "My grace is sufficient for you, for my power is made perfect in weakness." Therefore I will boast all the more gladly about my weaknesses, so that Christ's power may rest on me.
2 Corinthians 12:9 NIV

MAY 30

If a woman is to have the contentment and self-satisfaction necessary to produce a successful family, she needs the constant support and respect of the man she loves.

Dr. James Dobson, *What Wives Wish Their Husbands Knew about Women*, p. 162

For this reason a man will leave his father and mother and be united to his wife, and they will become one flesh. Genesis 2:24 NIV

AUGUST 3

The most vital objective of disciplining a child is to gain and maintain his respect. If the parents fail in this task, life becomes uncomfortable indeed.

Dr. James Dobson, *The New Dare to Discipline*, p. 30

Show proper respect to everyone.
1 Peter 2:17 NIV

$\mathcal{M}$AY 31

A child finds his greatest security in a structured environment where the rights of other people (and his own) are protected by definite boundaries.

Dr. James Dobson, *The Strong-Willed Child*, p. 30

I have chosen the way of truth; I have set my heart on your laws. I hold fast to your statutes, O LORD; do not let me be put to shame. I run in the path of your commands, for you have set my heart free. Psalm 119:30-32 NIV

AUGUST 2

Let me offer three phrases which will guide our parenting efforts during the final era of childhood. (1) Hold on with an open hand. (2) Hold them close and let them go. (3) If you love something set it free. If it comes back to you, then it's yours. If it doesn't return, it never was yours in the first place.

Dr. James Dobson, *The Strong-Willed Child,* p. 219

Whatever happens, conduct yourselves in a manner worthy of the gospel of Christ. Philippians 1:27 NIV

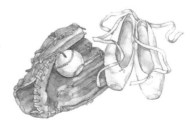

JUNE 1

Flattery occurs when you heap compliments upon a child for something he does not achieve, such as his or her beauty or clothing. Praise, on the other hand, is used to reinforce positive, constructive behavior.

Dr. James Dobson, *The New Dare to Discipline,* p. 96

Let us consider how we may spur one another on toward love and good deeds. . . . Let us encourage one another. Hebrews 10:24-25 NIV

AUGUST 1

There is no greater sense of self-esteem and personal worth than the personal awareness that comes from deeply ingrained spiritual values. Only Christ can provide the answers to questions such as: "Who am I?" "Who loves me?" "Where am I going?" and "What is the purpose of life?"

Dr. James Dobson, *Dr. Dobson Answers Your Questions*, p. 32

You are to give him the name Jesus, because he will save his people from their sins. Matthew 1:21 NIV

JUNE 2

I will consider my earthly existence to have been wasted unless I can recall a loving family, a consistent investment in the lives of people, and an earnest attempt to serve the God who made me.

Dr. James Dobson, *What Wives Wish Their Husbands Knew about Women,* p. 108

God has given each of you some special abilities; be sure to use them to help each other, passing on to others God's many kinds of blessings.
1 Peter 4:10 TLB

JULY 31

God has given us the assignment of representing Him during the formative years of parenting. That's why it is so critically important for us to acquaint our kids with God's two predominant natures, His unfathomable love and His justice.

Dr. James Dobson, *The New Dare to Discipline*, p. 19

We are therefore Christ's
ambassadors, as though God were
making his appeal through us.
2 Corinthians 5:20 NIV

JUNE 3

Husbands and wives should constantly guard against the scourge of overcommitment. Even worthwhile and enjoyable activities become damaging when they consume the last ounce of energy or the remaining free moments in the day.

Dr. James Dobson, *What Wives Wish Their Husbands Knew about Women,* p. 54

The mind controlled by the Spirit is life and peace.   Romans 8:6 NIV

JULY 30

God gave us a free choice because there is no significance
to love that knows no alternative.

Dr. James Dobson, *The Strong-Willed Child*, p. 221

I love those who love me, and those
who seek me find me.
                    Proverbs 8:17 NIV

JUNE 4

The parent-child relationship is the first and most important social interaction a youngster will have, and the flaws and knots experienced there can often be seen later in life.

Dr. James Dobson, *The New Dare to Discipline,* p. 18

Oh, that their hearts would be inclined to fear me and keep all my commands always, so that it might go well with them and their children forever! Deuteronomy 5:29 NIV

$\mathcal{J}$ULY 29

Anything that is considered desirable to an individual can serve as reinforcement for his behavior. Some children, for example, would rather receive a sincere word of praise than a ten-dollar bill, particularly if the adult approval is expressed in front of other children.

Dr. James Dobson, *Dare to Discipline,* p. 59

Pleasant words are a honeycomb,
sweet to the soul and healing to the
bones. Proverbs 16:24 NIV

JUNE 5

The Bible does not condemn an attitude of quiet self-respect and dignity. Jesus commanded us to love our neighbors as ourselves, implying not only that we are permitted a reasonable expression of dignity, but that love for others is impossible—until we experience a measure of self-respect.

Dr. James Dobson, *Dr. Dobson Answers Your Questions about Confident, Healthy Families,* p. 78

The second is: "You must love others as much as yourself." No other commandments are greater than these.　　Mark 12:31 TLB

JULY 28

Lasting love and affection often develop between people who have survived a crisis together.

Dr. James Dobson, *The New Dare to Discipline,* p. 234

Two can accomplish more than twice as much as one, for the results can be much better. If one falls, the other pulls him up; but if a man falls when he is alone, he's in trouble.

Ecclesiastes 4:9-10 TLB

JUNE 6

A relationship that is characterized by genuine love and affection is likely to be a healthy one, even though some parental mistakes and errors are inevitable.

Dr. James Dobson, *The Strong-Willed Child,* p. 33

Continue to show deep love for each other, for love makes up for many of your faults. 1 Peter 4:8 TLB

JULY 27

Love is more than a feeling—it also involves a commitment
of the will. You need an iron-fisted determination to make
your marriage succeed, which will act like the engine of a
train. It will keep you moving down the right track. On
the other hand, the feeling of love is like a caboose, being
pulled by the powerful engine at the other end.

Dr. James Dobson, *Preparing for Adolescence,* p. 117

*But if serving the LORD seems
undesirable to you, then choose for
yourselves this day whom you will
serve. . . . But as for me and my
household, we will serve the LORD.*
                    Joshua 24:15 NIV

JUNE 7

A child's attitude toward his parents' leadership is critical to his acceptance of their values and philosophy.

Dr. James Dobson, *The New Dare to Discipline,* p. 228

For God said, "Honor your father and mother." Matthew 15:4 NIV

JULY 26

The quickest way to destroy a romantic love between a husband and wife is for one partner to clamp a steel cage around the other.

Dr. James Dobson, *The Strong-Willed Child,* p. 220

You have been given freedom: not freedom to do wrong, but freedom to love and serve each other.
Galatians 5:13 TLB

JUNE 8

I cannot overemphasize the importance of instilling two distinct messages within your child before he is 48 months of age: (1) "I love you more than you can possibly understand." (2) "Because I love you, I must teach you to obey me. That is the only way I can take care of you and protect you from things that might hurt you."

Dr. James Dobson, *The Strong-Willed Child,* p. 52

Know then in your heart that as a man disciplines his son, so the LORD your God disciplines you.
Deuteronomy 8:5 NIV

JULY 25

There's no doubt about it: children are expensive little people. To raise them properly will require the very best that you can give of your time, effort, and financial resources.

Dr. James Dobson, *The Strong-Willed Child,* p. 8

Finally, be strong in the Lord and in his mighty power. Ephesians 6:10 NIV

JUNE 9

When properly applied, loving discipline works! It stimulates tender affection, made possible by mutual respect between a parent and a child. It bridges the gap that otherwise separates family members who should love and trust each other.

Dr. James Dobson, *The New Dare to Discipline,* p. 7

Those whom I love I rebuke and discipline. So be earnest, and repent. . . . I stand at the door and knock. If anyone hears my voice and opens the door, I will come in and eat with him, and he with me.
Revelation 3:19-20 NIV

$\mathcal{J}$ULY 24

Favorable attitudes which should be taught include
honesty, respect, kindness, love, human dignity,
obedience, responsibility, reverence. We can't instill
these attitudes during a brief, two-minute bedtime prayer.
We must *live* them from morning to night.

Dr. James Dobson, *The Strong-Willed Child,* p. 57

*Tie them on your finger, wear them
on your forehead, and write them on
the doorposts of your house!*
    Deuteronomy 6:8-9 TLB

JUNE 10

Kids can frustrate and irritate their parents . . . but the rewards of raising them far outweigh the cost. Besides, nothing worth having ever comes cheap.

Dr. James Dobson, *What Wives Wish Their Husbands Knew about Women,* p. 58

Everything comes from God alone.
Everything lives by his power, and
everything is for his glory.
Romans 11:36 TLB

JULY 23

There is a brief period during childhood when youngsters are vulnerable to religious training. Their concepts of right and wrong are formulated during this time, and their view of God begins to solidify.

Dr. James Dobson, *The New Dare to Discipline*, p. 232

Discipline your son in his early years while there is hope. If you don't you will ruin his life. Proverbs 19:18 TLB

JUNE 11

When a parent loses the early confrontations with the child, the later conflicts become harder to win. The parent who never wins, who is too weak or too tired to win, is making a costly mistake that will come back to haunt him during the child's adolescence.

Dr. James Dobson, *Dare to Discipline,* p. 21

Therefore, since we are surrounded by such a great cloud of witnesses, let us throw off everything that hinders and the sin that so easily entangles, and let us run with perseverance the race marked out for us. Let us fix our eyes on Jesus. Hebrews 12:1-2 NIV

JULY 22

By the time a child reaches four years of age, the focus of discipline should be not only on his behavior, but also on the attitudes which motivate it.

Dr. James Dobson, *The Strong-Willed Child,* p. 53

*Your attitudes and thoughts must all
be constantly changing for the better.*
Ephesians 4:23 TLB

JUNE 12

There is always room for more loving forgiveness within our homes.

Dr. James Dobson, *The New Dare to Discipline*, p. 67

Then Peter came to Jesus and asked,
"Lord, how many times shall I forgive
my brother when he sins against me?
Up to seven times?" Jesus answered,
"I tell you, not seven times, but
seventy-seven times."
               Matthew 18:21-22 NIV

JULY 21

You must keep a sense of humor during the twos and threes in order to preserve your own sanity. But you must also proceed with the task of instilling obedience and respect for authority.

Dr. James Dobson, *The Strong-Willed Child*, p. 51

As servants of God we commend ourselves in every way: . . . in purity, understanding, patience and kindness; in the Holy Spirit and in sincere love.

2 Corinthians 6:4, 6 NIV

JUNE 13

Let each member of the family know that the others value his viewpoint and opinion. Most important decisions should be shared within the group because that is an excellent way to build fidelity and family loyalty. However, the parents are the benevolent captains of the ship.

Dr. James Dobson, *Dr. Dobson Answers Your Questions,* p. 24

Teach me your way, O LORD, and I will walk in your truth.
Psalm 86:11 NIV

JULY 20

Disciplinary action is not an assault on parental love; it is a function of it. Appropriate punishment is not something parents do *to* a beloved child; it is something done *for* him or her.

Dr. James Dobson, *The New Dare to Discipline*, p. 22

Blessed is the man whom God corrects; so do not despise the discipline of the Almighty.
Job 5:17 NIV

$\mathcal{J}$UNE 14

If Christian parents are perceived by a child as not being worthy of respect, then neither is their religion, or their morals, or their government, or their country, or any of their values. This becomes the generation gap at its most basic level.

Dr. James Dobson, *Dare to Discipline*, p. 15

When arguing with a rebel, don't use foolish arguments as he does, or you will become as foolish as he is!
Proverbs 26:4 TLB

JULY 19

The *spirit* of a child is a million times more vulnerable than his will. It is a delicate flower that can be crushed and broken all too easily (and even unintentionally).

Dr. James Dobson, *The Strong-Willed Child,* p. 78

The wise in heart are called discerning, and pleasant words promote instruction.
Proverbs 16:21 NIV

JUNE 15

It is not difficult for some of us to believe that God is
capable of performing mighty deeds. . . . Having faith in
Him can be a fairly straightforward thing. To demonstrate
trust, however, takes the relationship a step farther. It
involves an element of risk. It requires us to depend on Him
to keep His promises, even when proof is not provided.

Dr. James Dobson, *When God Doesn't Make Sense*, p. 121

*This I declare, that he alone is my
refuge, my place of safety; he is my
God, and I am trusting him. For he
rescues you from every trap and
protects you from the fatal plague.*
Psalm 91:2-3 TLB

$\mathcal{J}$ULY 18

Children love justice. When someone has violated a rule, they want immediate retribution. They admire the teacher who can enforce an equitable legal system, and they find great comfort in reasonable school rules. By contrast, the teacher who does not control her class allows crime to pay, violating something basic in the value system of children.

Dr. James Dobson, *Dare to Discipline,* p. 106

This is what the Lord says: Do what is just and right. Rescue from the hand of his oppressor the one who has been robbed. Do no wrong or violence to the alien, the fatherless or the widow, and do not shed innocent blood in this place. Jeremiah 22:3 NIV

JUNE 16

Young children typically identify their parents . . . and especially their fathers . . . with God.

Dr. James Dobson, *The New Dare to Discipline*, p. 19

*I will be a Father to you, and you will
be my sons and daughters, says the
Lord Almighty.*
2 Corinthians 6:18 NIV

JULY 17

Overprotection produces emotional cripples who often develop lasting characteristics of dependency and a kind of perpetual adolescence.

Dr. James Dobson, *The Strong-Willed Child*, p. 62

God sometimes uses sorrow in our lives to help us turn away from sin and seek eternal life. We should never regret his sending it.
2 Corinthians 7:10 TLB

JUNE 17

Adult leadership is rarely accepted unchallenged by the next generation; it must be "tested" and found worthy of allegiance by the youngsters who are asked to yield and submit to its direction.

Dr. James Dobson, *The Strong-Willed Child,* p. 15

Submit yourselves, then, to God. Resist the devil, and he will flee from you. Come near to God and he will come near to you. James 4:7-8 NIV

JULY 16

The task of parenting is too scary on our own, and there is not enough knowledge on the books to guarantee the outcome of our parenting duties. We desperately need divine help with the job!

Dr. James Dobson, *The New Dare to Discipline,* p. 247

If any of you lack wisdom, let him ask of God, that giveth to all men liberally, and upbraideth not; and it shall be given him. James 1:5 KJV

JUNE 18

Dr. Fitzhugh Dodson stated in his book *How to Father* that your child "needs time with you when you are not demanding anything from him, time when the two of you are mutually enjoying yourselves." I agree!

Dr. James Dobson, *Dr. Dobson Answers Your Questions about Raising Children*, p. 137

So I commend the enjoyment of life, because nothing is better for a man under the sun than to eat and drink and be glad. Then joy will accompany him in his work all the days of the life God has given him under the sun. Ecclesiastes 8:15 NIV

$\mathcal{J}$ULY 15

A good marriage is not one where perfection reigns; it is a relationship where a healthy perspective overlooks a multitude of "unresolvables."

Dr. James Dobson, *What Wives Wish Their Husbands Knew about Women,* p. 185

May you rejoice in the wife of your youth. Proverbs 5:18 NIV

JUNE 19

Like a father leading his trusting child, our Lord will guide our steps and teach us his wisdom.

Dr. James Dobson, *Dr. Dobson Answers Your Questions,* p. 482

I will bless the Lord who counsels me; he gives me wisdom in the night. He tells me what to do. Psalm 16:7 TLB

JULY 14

There will be times when God's behavior will be
incomprehensible and confusing to us.

Dr. James Dobson, *Dr. Dobson Answers Your Questions*, p. 486

My thoughts are not your thoughts,
neither are your ways my ways, saith
the Lord.   Isaiah 55:8 KJV

JUNE 20

Parental warmth after discipline is essential to demonstrate that it is the *behavior*—not the child himself—that the parent rejects.

Dr. James Dobson, *The New Dare to Discipline,* p. 36

I will heal their waywardness and love them freely, for my anger has turned away from them.
Hosea 14:4 NIV

JULY 13

Parents often use anger to get action instead of using action to get action. It is exhausting and it doesn't work! Trying to control children by screaming is as utterly futile as trying to steer a car by honking the horn.

Dr. James Dobson, *The New Dare to Discipline,* p. 36

A soft answer turneth away wrath:
but grievous words stir up anger.
Proverbs 15:1 KJV

JUNE 21

Our heavenly Father is a God of unlimited love. . . . But our Lord is also the possessor of majestic authority! The universe is ordered by the supreme Lord who requires obedience from his children and has warned them that "the wages of sin is death." To show our little ones love without authority is as serious a distortion of God's nature as to reveal an iron-fisted authority without love.

Dr. James Dobson, *Dr. Dobson Answers Your Questions about Raising Children*, p. 37

God is both kind and severe.
Romans 11:22 TLB

JULY 12

We will be unable to teach appreciativeness if we never say "please" or "thank you" at home. We will not produce honest children if we teach them to lie to the bill collector on the phone by saying, "Dad's not home."

Dr. James Dobson, *The Strong-Willed Child*, p. 56

Be very careful, then, how you live—not as unwise but as wise.
Ephesians 5:15 NIV

JUNE 22

If there is one word most often heard from children
between fifteen and twenty-four months of age, it is *"No!"*

Dr. James Dobson, *The Strong-Willed Child,* p. 42

*When I was a child, I talked like
a child, I thought like a child, I
reasoned like a child.*
　　　　　1 Corinthians 13:11 NIV

Parents should be deeply involved in the lives of their young children, providing love and protection and authority. But when those children reach their late teens and early twenties, the cage door must be opened to the world outside.

Dr. James Dobson, *The Strong-Willed Child,* p. 219

He shielded him and cared for him; he guarded him as the apple of his eye, like an eagle that stirs up its nest and hovers over its young, that spreads its wings to catch them and carries them on its pinions.
Deuteronomy 32:10-11 NIV

JUNE 23

Life has enough crises in it without magnifying our troubles during good times, yet peace of mind is often surrendered for such insignificant causes.

Dr. James Dobson, *The New Dare to Discipline*, p. 246

Who of you by worrying can add a single hour to his life?
Matthew 6:27 NIV

$\mathcal{J}$ULY 10

Because mothers and fathers represent "God" to their children, the fundamental element in teaching morality can be achieved through a healthy parental relationship during the early years.

Dr. James Dobson, *The New Dare to Discipline,* p. 228

Blessed are they whose ways are blameless, who walk according to the law of the LORD.   Psalm 119:1 NIV

JUNE 24

A spanking is to be reserved for use in response to willful defiance rather than mere childish irresponsibility.

Dr. James Dobson, *The Strong-Willed Child,* p. 36

Do not resent it when God chastens and corrects you, for his punishment is proof of his love. Proverbs 3:11 TLB

JULY 9

The Lord will not save a person against his will, but He has a thousand ways of making him more willing. Our prayers unleash the power of God in the life of another individual. We have been granted the privilege of entering into intercessory prayer for our loved ones and of holding their names and faces before the Father.

Dr. James Dobson, *When God Doesn't Make Sense,* p. 201

Pray for one another. . . . The effectual fervent prayer of a righteous man availeth much.   James 5:16 KJV

JUNE 25

It is helpful to understand that emotions are cyclical in nature. . . . [Depression] is likely to appear following a busy holiday, the birth of a baby, a job promotion, or even after a restful vacation. . . . Highs must be followed by lows. But in the healthy individual lows eventually give way to highs, too.

Dr. James Dobson, *What Wives Wish Their Husbands Knew about Women*, p. 19

O my soul, why be so gloomy and discouraged? Trust in God! I shall again praise him for his wondrous help; he will make me smile again, for he is my God! Psalm 43:5 TLB

JULY 8

A parent, teacher, scoutmaster, or recreation leader who tries to control a group of children by use of his own anger is due for a long, long day of frustration.

Dr. James Dobson, *Dare to Discipline,* p. 28

Dear brothers, don't ever forget that it is best to listen much, speak little, and not become angry.
James 1:19 TLB

JUNE 26

Give your child an exposure to responsibility and work, but preserve time for play and fun.

Dr. James Dobson, *The New Dare to Discipline,* p. 155

To every thing there is a season, and a time to every purpose under the heaven: . . . A time to weep, and a time to laugh; a time to mourn, and a time to dance. Ecclesiastes 3:1, 4 KJV

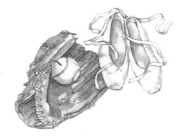

JULY 7

There is no substitute for parental modeling of the attitudes we wish to teach. Someone wrote, "The footsteps a child follows are most likely to be the ones his parents thought they covered up."

Dr. James Dobson, *The Strong-Willed Child,* p. 56

Prompted by her mother, she said, "Give me here on a platter the head of John the Baptist."
Matthew 14:8 NIV

 JUNE 27

After age 13 to 16, some adolescents resent being told
exactly what to believe; they do not want religion "forced
down their throats," and should be given more and more
autonomy in what they believe. If the early exposure has
been properly conducted, they will have an inner
mainstay to steady them.

Dr. James Dobson, *Dr. Dobson Answers Your Questions,* p. 55

*If they fall it isn't fatal, for the Lord
holds them with his hand.*
Psalm 37:24 TLB

JULY 6

Some babies seem determined to dismantle the homes into which they were born. But from that demanding tyrant will grow a thinking, loving human being with an eternal soul and a special place in the heart of the Creator.

Dr. James Dobson, *The Strong-Willed Child*, p. 40

*Overlook my youthful sins, O Lord!
Look at me instead through eyes of
mercy and forgiveness, through eyes
of everlasting love and kindness.*
Psalm 25:6-7 TLB

JUNE 28

It is very difficult to separate basic human worth from the quality of one's own body. The pressure is greatly magnified in a highly eroticized society such as ours. Those with the least sex appeal necessarily begin to worry about their ability to compete in the marketplace. They feel bankrupt in the most valuable "currency" of the day.

Dr. James Dobson, *What Wives Wish Their Husbands Knew about Women*, pp. 26–27

As God's messenger I give each of you God's warning: Be honest in your estimate of yourselves, measuring your value by how much faith God has given you. Romans 12:3 TLB

JULY 5

Parents should begin talking to their children at length while they are still babies. Interesting mobiles and winking-blinking toys should be arranged around the crib. From then on through the toddler years, learning activities should be programmed regularly.

Dr. James Dobson, *The New Dare to Discipline,* p. 180

Watch yourselves closely so that you do not forget the things your eyes have seen or let them slip from your heart as long as you live. Teach them to your children.

Deuteronomy 4:9 NIV

JUNE 29

The best way to get children to do what you want is to spend time with them before disciplinary problems occur—having fun together and enjoying mutual laughter and joy. When those moments of love and closeness happen, kids are not as tempted to challenge and test the limits.

Dr. James Dobson, *The New Dare to Discipline,* p. 75

If you have any encouragement from being united with Christ, if any comfort from his love, if any fellowship with the Spirit, if any tenderness and compassion, then make my joy complete by being like-minded, having the same love, being one in spirit and purpose.
Philippians 2:1-2 NIV

JULY 4

Independence Day

The great value of traditions is that they give a family a sense of identity and belonging. All of us desperately need to feel that . . . we're a family that's conscious of our uniqueness, our character, and our heritage. That feeling is the only antidote for the loneliness and isolation that characterize so many homes today.

Dr. James Dobson, *Dr. Dobson Answers Your Questions about Raising Children,* p. 23

This is a day you are to commemorate; for the generations to come you shall celebrate it as a festival to the Lord—a lasting ordinance.
Exodus 12:14 NIV

JUNE 30

This is the beauty of committed love—that which is avowed to be a lifelong devotion. A man and a woman can then face the good and the bad times together as friends and allies.

Dr. James Dobson, *What Wives Wish Their Husbands Knew about Women,* p. 176

Let us not become weary in doing good, for at the proper time we will reap a harvest if we do not give up.
Galatians 6:9 NIV

JULY 3

It is important to spank *immediately* after the offense, or not at all. A toddler's memory is not sufficiently developed to permit even a ten-minute delay in the administration of justice.

Dr. James Dobson, *The Strong-Willed Child*, p. 47

Folly is bound up in the heart of a child, but the rod of discipline will drive it far from him.

Proverbs 22:15 NIV

$\mathscr{J}$ULY 1

Canada Day

A vital fringe benefit of being a Christian is the
tremendous sense of identity that grows out of knowing
Jesus Christ.

Dr. James Dobson, *Dr. Dobson Answers Your Questions, p. 32*

*Lord, you have assigned me my
portion and my cup; you have made
my lot secure.*   Psalm 16:5 NIV

JULY 2

It is my belief that the weakening of America's financial position in the world and the difficulties its families and children are experiencing can be traced to our departure from traditional values and Biblical concepts of morality.

Dr. James Dobson, *The New Dare to Discipline,* p. 236

All have turned aside, they have together become corrupt; there is no one who does good, not even one.
Psalm 14:3 NIV